Excellence *in* Ministry

A Study of 1 Timothy

BIBLE STUDY GUIDE

From the Bible-teaching ministry of

Charles R. Swindoll

INSIGHT FOR LIVING

Chuck graduated in 1963 from Dallas Theological Seminary, where he now serves as the school's fourth president, helping to prepare a new generation of men and women for the ministry. Chuck has served in pastorates in three states: Massachusetts, Texas, and California, including almost twenty-three years at the First Evangelical Free Church in Fullerton, California. His sermon messages have been aired over radio since 1979 as the *Insight for Living* broadcast. A best-selling author, Chuck has written numerous books and booklets on many subjects.

Based on the outlines and transcripts of Chuck's sermons, the study guide text is co-authored by Gary Matlack, a graduate of Texas Tech University and Dallas Theological Seminary. He also wrote the Living Insights sections.

Editor in Chief:
Cynthia Swindoll

Coauthor of Text:
Gary Matlack

Assistant Editor:
Wendy Peterson

Copy Editor:
Tom Kimber

Text Designer:
Gary Lett

Publishing System Specialist:
Alex Pasieka

Director, Communications Division:
Deedee Snyder

Marketing Manager:
Alene Cooper

Project Coordinator:
Colette Muse

Production Manager:
John Norton

Printer:
Sinclair Printing Company

Unless otherwise identified, all Scripture references are from the New American Standard Bible, © The Lockman Foundation 1960, 1962, 1963, 1968, 1971, 1972, 1973, 1975, 1977. Used by permission. Scripture taken from the Holy Bible, New International Version © 1973, 1978, 1984 International Bible Society, used by permission of Zondervan Bible Publishers. The other translation cited is *The New Testament in Modern English* [PHILLIPS].

An effort has been made to locate sources and obtain permission where necessary for the quotations used in this book. In the event of any unintentional omission, a modification will gladly be incorporated in future printings.

ISBN 0-8499-8651-6

COVER DESIGN: Nina Paris

COVER PAINTING: *The Miracle of St. Paul at Ephesus* by Jean I. Restout. Musee des Beaux-Arts, Rouen, France. Courtesy of Giraudon/Art Resource, New York.

Printed in the United States of America

CONTENTS

INTRODUCTION

During my pastorate at First Evangelical Free Church in Fullerton, I admitted to my congregation how much I loved the ministry . . . *and* how committed I was to them personally. As a pastor who stood before the same flock week after week, I was grateful that God had not left us in the dark when it came to understanding and maintaining the work of ministry.

Realizing the inestimable value of His counsel recorded in the first letter Paul wrote Timothy, I dug deeply into each chapter and discovered anew what the ministry is all about. With so many voices and various models thrown at us these days, it's easy to be confused, isn't it? I decided it would be most beneficial to hear again what *God* has to say about ministry.

This series is the result of that study—a verse-by-verse analysis of 1 Timothy. Hopefully, you'll find it neither tedious nor needlessly dogmatic but rather a balanced, reasonable approach you can live with and carry out. May greater excellence occur in all of our ministries as a result of our coming to terms with these truths!

Chuck Swindoll

Chuck Swindoll

Putting Truth into Action

Knowledge apart from application falls short of God's desire for His children. He wants us to apply what we learn so that we will change and grow. This study guide was prepared with these goals in mind. As you go through the following pages, we hope your desire to discover biblical truth will grow as your understanding of God's Word increases and that you will be encouraged to apply what you've learned.

To assist you in your study, we've included a section called **Living Insights** at the end of each lesson. These exercises will challenge you to study further and to think of specific ways to put your discoveries into action.

On occasion a lesson is followed by a **Digging Deeper** section, which gives you additional information and resources to probe further into some issues raised in that lesson.

There are many ways to use this guide—in personal devotions, group studies, discussions with friends and family, and Sunday school classes. And, of course, it's an ideal study aid when you're listening to its corresponding *Insight for Living* radio series.

To benefit most from this study guide, we would encourage you to consider it a spiritual journal. That's why we've included space in the **Living Insights** for recording your thoughts and discoveries. We hope you'll return to those sections often for review and encouragement as you continue to grow in your walk with Christ.

Gary Matlack
Coauthor of Text
Author of Living Insights

Excellence
in
Ministry

A Study of 1 Timothy

EXCELLENCE IN MINISTRY
The Ministry as God Intended It

Writer: Paul (1:1)
Recipient: Timothy (1:2)
Message: Correct belief and behavior for the pastor and his flock (3:14–15)
Date: Circa A.D. 64–65

"Grace, mercy and peace . . ." (1:2)

"Grace be with you" (6:21)

	Greeting and Salutation	PERSONAL ENCOURAGEMENT AND EXHORTATION	THE MINISTRY	THE MINISTER	
	1:1–2	1:3 1:20	2:1 3:16	4:1 6:21	

PERSONAL ENCOURAGEMENT AND EXHORTATION
- Timothy's Task
- Paul's Testimony
- Gospel's Trust

THE MINISTRY
Chapter 2 Men and Women
- Prayer and Submission

Chapter 3 Elders and Deacons
- Qualifications
- Leadership

THE MINISTER
Chapter 4 Seeing the Importance of
- Faithful Teaching
- Sound Doctrine
- True Godliness
- Perseverance

Chapter 5 Paying Attention to
- Various Age Groups
- Widows
- Elders
- Wisdom

Chapter 6 Maintaining Balance with
- Masters and Slaves
- Internals and Externals
- Rich and Poor

	EMPHASIS	COMMAND
THE WORK OF MINISTRY	BE TRUE!	
	BE WISE!	
THE ONE WHO MINISTERS		
BE STRONG AND FAITHFUL		

EMPHASIS

COMMAND

"MUSICAL" INTERLUDES

Chapter 1

THE CHURCH AS GOD PLANNED IT

A Survey of 1 Timothy

No one can arrange your house the way you can.

You are the sole architect of its ambience, creating a desired feel and specific personality for each room. The leather wing chair, the brick fireplace, and the brass floor lamp that warms the living room with a gentle splash of light all say, "Sit here; read; relax." In the guest bathroom, fresh towels—white, navy, burgundy, forest green—hang like flags welcoming a visiting dignitary. The master bedroom, fragrant with potpourri and cushioned with comforter, pillows, and plump curtains, suggests that there is no softer or sweeter place on earth to sleep.

Now imagine someone barging into your home and rearranging everything—totally disregarding your personal design, creative flair, and knowledge of what works best for your family. Unthinkable!

Yet how often do we "rearrange" God's household—the church —which He has already set up according to His plan? He has given us guidelines for teaching, criteria for selecting leadership, and in-structions for meeting people's needs. Many Christians, however, fumble frantically through ministry without noticing or appreciating God's design. They throw together programs, muscle people into service, and replace ministry essentials with man-made options. Let's take a look at just how far today's church has departed from the divine design.

Some Observations about the Church Today

The church at the end of the twentieth century has "rearranged" God's household in at least four ways.

1

- **First: There is a deeper commitment to tradition than to Scripture.**

Rigidity rules in many congregations. "We've always done it that way," echoes through the halls of tradition-bound churches, squelching any whimper of innovation or creativity.

Nothing is wrong with tradition, per se. It reminds us of our roots and our heritage and provides opportunities for celebration and reflection. But we go too far when we make tradition, and not the Scriptures, our primary yardstick for measuring ministry.

Tradition rules in churches that haven't studied the Bible deeply enough to distinguish absolutes from nonabsolutes. The Word is clear about what God expects of His church, but it also allows room for creativity. How else could the church fit into various cultures and adapt to changing technology? Scripture, not tradition, is the final word on how to conduct ourselves in the household of God.

- **Second: Many churches care more about being successful by the world's standard than about modeling New Testament values.**

Disregard for the Bible's instruction on the church can lead not only to traditionalism but to secularism—adoption of the world's standard for success.

In the world arena, bigger and flashier is better. So we attend motivational seminars on how to market and promote church growth. Instead of depending on the Spirit to draw people, we use all sorts of bells and whistles to wow them. We abandon the slow, steady climb of discipleship for the roller coaster ride of big business and entertainment. As a result, we turn ministers into managers; clergy into CEOs; shepherds into showmen.

- **Third: The church is larger than ever but more confused and uncertain.**

"Preach the Word at home and abroad." At one time the church's top priority seemed to boil down to that simple statement. But try rallying around that cry today.

The vision of most churches is fuzzy. The messages coming out of many pulpits sound more like pop psychology than preaching; more human-centered than God-centered. They exalt our self-esteem rather than magnify the Lord. Having lost their grasp on the church's central message and mission, many Christian leaders work themselves into an early grave . . . and don't even know why. This study is intended to help us find our way.

- **Fourth: We are polarized by labels rather than unified by love.**

We would feel lost without labels, wouldn't we? Categories help us size up those who don't agree with us; they protect us from those in the "enemy" theological camp.

Jesus, however, envisioned something different for His church —a unified body (look up John 17:20–23). The worldwide church of Jesus Christ is sprinkled throughout a variety of denominations and independent churches. And we're all related through Him. But too often, we fail to love one another as He has loved us.

Does that mean we should compromise the gospel or surrender our convictions in order to get along? No. But we shouldn't let differences in nonessentials keep us from loving and interacting with others who also know and love Christ.

To restore excellence to ministry, we need to abide by God's design for His household. And this isn't for just the pastor or church planter. If you know Christ, you're in ministry. So let's pay closer attention to God's original blueprint, and give less consideration to our handwritten revisions.

Background of 1 Timothy

The letter of 1 Timothy glows with the flame of a torch passing from the apostle Paul's hand to that of his friend and protégé, Timothy, whom he had known for perhaps as many as twenty years. It is one of three "pastoral epistles"—2 Timothy and Titus are the other two. Personal in nature, these letters were written to individuals who, like the apostle, were intimately acquainted with the daily grind of ministry. All three were penned near the end of Paul's life.

What do you tell your understudy when you realize your time is almost up? What else but the things closest to your heart. For Paul, that meant the purity of the gospel and the development of Christ's church. So he wrote to Timothy to deepen him in the message and ministry of the church, God's household (1 Tim. 3:15).

An Overview of 1 Timothy

Let's get acquainted with this letter by seeing the big picture. A view of how it fits together and a feel for its flow will help us understand the content.

As you can see on the chart at the beginning of this guide, the letter divides into three main sections. Chapter 1 focuses on Paul's *personal encouragement and exhortation* to Timothy. Chapters 2 and 3 emphasize *the ministry*. And chapters 4 through 6 deal with *the minister*.

Chapter 1: Personal Encouragement and Exhortation

Immediately after Paul's opening greeting (1:1–2), notice his first exhortation: "remain on at Ephesus" (v. 3).[1] Paul is saying, "Stay at it, Timothy. Keep building up and strengthening the community at Ephesus." Perhaps Timothy felt intimidated by the task of trying to provide leadership for the early church. Or maybe he was weary of defending the faith against false teachers (see vv. 3–4).

Paul, however, urges him to stay and preach the true Word to counteract fruitless and destructive doctrines (vv. 3–11). This involves more than simply distributing knowledge, though. "The goal," writes Paul, "is love" (v. 5), which flows from a clean conscience and a genuine faith.

As Paul's life testified, the gospel is the only message that can make the godless godly (vv. 12–17). Paul concludes this section by reminding Timothy that the Good News of Christ must remain the focus of his ministry. That's the only way to avoid the spiritual shipwreck suffered by others who failed to keep "faith and a good conscience" (vv. 18–20).

Chapters 2 and 3: The Ministry

This section first emphasizes the priority of prayer. Rather than prescribing a regimen, Paul addresses prayer's scope and spirit. He wants all Christians to unite in prayer for all people, and especially for those in authority (vv. 1–2, 8).

Then he reiterates the gospel, stressing that Christ Jesus is the only mediator between God and humanity (vv. 3–7).

What about women in ministry? Paul handles this theological hot potato in verses 9–15, including instruction on outer appearance, inner spirituality, and roles in the church.

Chapter 3 is indispensable in choosing church leaders. Without these guidelines for elders (vv. 1–7) and deacons (vv. 8–13), we would gravitate toward the most dominant personalities, the most charismatic people. The church, then, would be no different from

---

1. Even the best ministers think about leaving from time to time. Today, the average tenure for a pastor at one church is four years. See George Barna, *Today's Pastors* (Ventura, Calif.: Gospel Light, Regal Books, 1993), p. 36.

the world. But character, Paul points out, is the primary issue in selecting shepherds for the flock.

And in verses 14–16, Paul states his purpose for writing: to instruct Timothy on proper conduct in the household of God (vv. 14–16).

Chapters 4 through 6: The Minister

Paul now turns from the work of the ministry to the life of the minister. He reminds Timothy that some will fall away from the faith and teach false doctrine (4:1–5). But the apostle urges his friend to avoid that end by practicing self-discipline (vv. 6–8), prescribing the truth and giving ideas for its application (vv. 9–11), and modeling perseverance (vv. 12–16).

In chapter 5, Paul instructs Timothy on how to build relationships and minister to specific groups within the church—men (v. 1); women (v. 2); widows (vv. 3–16); and elders (vv. 17–20). This chapter concludes with exhortations to practice discernment in everything from choosing leadership to enhancing good health (vv. 21–25).

After urging slaves and masters to live in Christian harmony (6:1–2), Paul tells Timothy to focus on the right things in ministry: the truth over false doctrine (vv. 3–5); contentment over greed (vv. 6–10); the spiritual over the material (vv. 11–16); and giving over greed (vv. 17–19). The letter closes with a final charge to teach the truth of the gospel (vv. 20–21).

Several Contrasts Worth Considering

This letter brings opposites together, melding contrasting ideas into balanced principles that we need to keep in mind.

First, we desire a twentieth-century ministry based on first-century principles. God's truth doesn't change, but times do. So do styles and methods. We need to remain rooted in the Scriptures but stay in touch with our culture.

Second, there will always be tension between scriptural ideals and human realities. While striving to be all God wants us to be, we must realize that perfection eludes us this side of heaven. So let's urge each other on to godliness but allow room for failure and brokenness.

Third, truth is truth, whether it's modeled or not. Though he encouraged Timothy to live out the reality of his faith, Paul realized that Christianity would not fall if Timothy did. The pages of church history are strewn with defectors. But God's Word never fails.

Fourth, regardless of the church's weaknesses, it will not fail. Not because of us, but because of Jesus Christ, who said, "I will build My church; and the gates of Hades shall not overpower it" (Matt. 16:18b). We have the privilege of participating in the building of God's kingdom. But the project will succeed because of His perfect faithfulness, not ours.

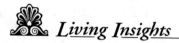 ## Living Insights

Since 1 Timothy was written by an apostle to another Christian leader about ministry, you might wonder how it can affect you if you're not a pastor, church planter, elder, or some type of ministry "professional."

Well, take heart. Paul's letter can benefit all believers. For example, we all need sound doctrine in order to distinguish false teaching from the true gospel. And, if you're a woman who's wondering how to fit into the ministry of a local church, that topic is also addressed. If you ever want to serve as an elder or deacon, or if you're ever asked to vote on church officers, you need to know God's standards for those positions. How do we minister to the lonely and destitute? How should we look at money? This study will touch all of these topics.

Are you wrestling with one or more of these issues right now? Why not take some time to read through 1 Timothy, perhaps more than once. Then, as topics come to mind you would like to explore in depth, write them down. Look ahead to see which study guide chapters cover those topics. Before reading that chapter, take some time to prepare. Come up with some specific questions. Use a concordance or Bible dictionary to find out what other passages say about the same topic. Then, when you're ready to read that chapter, you'll be set for an extra enriching study built around your particular needs at this point in life.

Topics I want to explore: _____

Right conduct & right teaching

_____

_____

Other passages to consider: _____

_____

_____

_____

Specific questions I need answered: _____

_____

_____

_____

Here's to a rewarding time in the Word!

 ## *Digging Deeper*

Although God has given us His instructions for setting up and running His "household," He still gives us freedom to add our own touch—as long as we don't change the essentials of His original design. As you move through this study, ask yourself, "What am I free to change, and what must I not tamper with?"

Here's an example of how that question will help. First Timothy 3:1–7 assumes that there will be elders in the church and lists their qualifications. This tells us that churches need leaders with godly character. But how many do we need? What should the proportion of elders to members be? How often should they meet? You see, we have some freedom to work out certain issues ourselves.

The secret to good Bible study is to extract timeless principles that apply to any culture in any time. Once we do that, we can get creative. But first, we need to distinguish the timeless from the time-bound. Keep that in mind as you study.

Chapter 2

WHAT'S A PASTOR TO DO?

1 Timothy 1:1–11, 18–20

WANTED:

Minister for a Growing Church

Must have experience as shepherd, CEO, office manager, educator, salesman, diplomat, referee, writer, theologian, politician, motivational speaker, Boy Scout leader, psychologist, social worker, funeral director, wedding consultant, master of ceremonies, church planter, missionary. Helpful but not essential: landscape manager, interior decorator, musician, minor league athlete, stand-up comedian.

Should have answers to life's tough questions about suffering, dying, God's sovereignty. Must hold firm convictions on every topic, but not allowed to ruffle anyone's feathers. Must think as deeply as C. S. Lewis, preach as passionately as C. H. Spurgeon, listen as sensitively as James Dobson.

Sweet disposition required at all times, even when attacked or simply having a bad day. Must have wisdom and experience of age but energy and glow of youth. Required to attend every potluck dinner, yet remain slim. Twenty-four-hour-a-day availability a must (beeper provided). Must spend quality time with family.

Applicant's wife must be both stunning and plain, quiet yet outgoing. She should keep home immaculate but be available to teach Sunday school, organize socials, and disciple women. Applicant's children must be exemplary in conduct and character, yet no different from other kids; dressed decently.

Salary not commensurate with experience or need; no overtime pay; frequent criticism. Non-smoking, non-dancing, non-movie-viewing environment. An equal opportunity employer.[1]

---

1. Adapted from "Minister Wanted," in *Kethiv Qere* (school paper of Dallas Theological Seminary), March 26, 1975.

OK. Maybe you've never seen a want ad quite like that. But ask around and you might be surprised at what some people think pastors are supposed to do . . . and be.

That's one reason Paul wrote to Timothy—to clear up confusion about the duties, expectations, and priorities of the ministry. And that instruction was necessary in the emerging church of the first century.

False doctrines—such as the denial of Christ's deity, the rejection of His humanity, and salvation by works—abounded in the sphere of Timothy's ministry. That's why this letter mandates preaching the truth. Timothy, however, must have felt overwhelmed at times as he tried to extinguish the theological and administrative fires that flared up in Ephesus, plus provide some kind of structure to a church growing by leaps and bounds.

The demands of ministry in our times, just as in Timothy's, are greater than our ability to meet them all. So we need a guidebook to help us distinguish the crucial from the secondary, the eternal from the temporal. First Timothy is such a guidebook. And Paul, the author of this letter, is our guide.

Warm Words to a Close Friend

> Paul, an apostle of Christ Jesus according to the commandment of God our Savior, and of Christ Jesus, who is our hope. (1 Tim. 1:1)

Apostle. That one word tells us Paul was hand picked by God for ministry. He was seasoned, scarred, well-traveled, and wise. He felt the sharp blows of stones hurled at him and winced under the slashing fury of a whip. In some towns, people wanted to worship him as a god. In others, he was thrown into prison for preaching the gospel. He had known success, suffering, encouragement, and abandonment.

So this letter doesn't come to us from the hallowed halls of academia or the stale study of some theologian removed from the mainstream. Paul's pen writes, not only with the ink of sound doctrine, but with the blood, sweat, and tears of an experienced minister.

What was Paul like? One ancient source, *The Acts of Paul and Thecla,* written about A.D. 200, describes the apostle this way:

> [Paul was] a man of little stature, thin-haired upon the head, crooked in the legs, of good state of body, with eyebrows meeting, and with nose somewhat

hooked, full of grace, for sometimes he appeared like
a man and sometimes he had the face of an angel.[2]

By the time he wrote to Timothy, what little hair Paul had left
was probably gray or white. Most likely, he didn't get around as
well as he used to. He knew his days were numbered. So he needed
someone younger to carry the torch of Christ's ministry, and his
thoughts ran to his dear friend Timothy.

To Timothy, my true child in the faith: Grace, mercy
and peace from God the Father and Christ Jesus our
Lord. (v. 2)

Paul and Timothy's relationship resembled that of a father and
son. Paul took Timothy under his wing at Lystra (Acts 16:1–3),
and taught, discipled, and encouraged him. Eventually, Timothy
proved himself capable of representing Paul and succeeding him in
ministry (see 1 Cor. 4:17; Phil. 2:19; 1 Thess. 3:2).

What an encouragement this letter must have been to Timothy.
As he unrolled the parchment and began to read Paul's words,
memories of their years of ministry together surely swept across his
mind. Paul's letter reassured Timothy that, though he may have felt
overwhelmed at times, he wasn't alone. His heavenly Father, as well
as his "spiritual father," were there to provide comfort and strength.

By the way, the ministry can be a lonely profession. To develop
the character and walk with God necessary to serve others, solitude
is a must. Plus, those who minister sometimes have to stand alone
and risk losing popularity. That's why we all need someone we can
open up to; someone who understands. Someone like Paul or Timothy.

Wise Counsel from a Seasoned Veteran

In this first section of Paul's letter, we can distill his advice into
five directives: stay at the task, communicate the truth, concentrate
on the target, remember the standard, and obey the command.

Stay at the Task

Notice the first command: "remain on at Ephesus" (1 Tim. 1:3a).
Don't be fooled—ministers think about quitting their jobs, just like

2. William Barclay, *The Letters to the Corinthians*, rev. ed., The Daily Study Bible Series
(Philadelphia, Pa.: Westminster Press, 1975), pp. 242–43.

anyone else. The pressure's intense, the people often inflexible, and the expectations unreasonable. And sometimes it *is* best to move on.

But more often than not, the best thing to do is stay at it. Persevere. And let God forge His glory in the furnace of ministry. There is no such thing as stress-free or problem-proof ministry. If the grass is greener on the other side, you can bet their water bill is higher.

Communicate the Truth

As if Paul anticipates the question, "Why should I stay here in Ephesus?" from Timothy, he quickly supplies the answer:

> in order that you may instruct certain men not to teach strange doctrines, nor to pay attention to myths and endless genealogies, which give rise to mere speculation rather than furthering the admin-istration of God which is by faith. (vv. 3b–4)

The phrase "in order that" begins a purpose clause explaining why Timothy should stay. What's the reason? To paraphrase Paul, "To answer false doctrine with true doctrine." Interesting, isn't it, that the first topic Paul brings up is sound doctrine. That theme also closes the letter (6:20–21) and recurs throughout it (4:1–7; 6:3–5).

Paul saw communication of the truth as the top priority in Timothy's ministry. A fluffy familiarity with Christian lingo wasn't enough, because the claims of Christ were being assaulted by men teaching "strange doctrines" (1:3b). This phrase, according to com-mentator Philip H. Towner,

> literally means "different doctrines" (compare 6:3), those that diverged from the accepted teaching of the Old Testament, Christ and the apostles.[3]

Paul doesn't elaborate on the details of these doctrines, but he says they involve "myths and endless genealogies" (1:4a). According to commentator Duane Litfin,

> They may have had a Gnostic flavor, but were more likely of Jewish origin (cf. Titus 1:14). Whatever their nature, they were empty of any spiritual value

---

3. Philip H. Towner, *1–2 Timothy and Titus*, The IVP New Testament Commentary Series (Downers Grove, Ill.: InterVarsity Press, 1994), p. 44.

and led only to further speculation, questions, and arguments. Such speculations were to be avoided because they did not further God's plan, which is grasped and implemented not by human imaginings, but by faith. By contrast, human speculations tend to lead off down endless blind tunnels which serve only to confuse and obscure God's truth.[4]

Gnosticism taught that all matter, including the body, was evil. Gnostics, then, denied Jesus' incarnation. On the other hand, one variety of Judaism taught that an individual must observe all the Jewish traditions to be saved—in addition to trusting in Christ (see Acts 15). Timothy had to weed out such false doctrines as they crept into the church.

Also, Ephesus itself was the center of worship for the goddess Artemis, whose temple was considered one of the seven wonders of the world in its day.[5] Knowing and teaching God's Word wasn't an option in this city; it was a necessity.

And it still is a necessity today. We're seated before a buffet of false teachings; many of them attractive, some even sprinkled with a few grains of truth. That's why all of us, not just pastors, need to know God's Word well enough to discern the false from the true. Otherwise, we'll swallow anything, even the tasty but poisonous fare offered by cults.

Concentrate on the Target

We don't, however, accumulate knowledge just to win arguments with false teachers. Christian truth does more than satisfy the mind, as Paul makes clear:

> But the goal of our instruction is love from a pure heart and a good conscience and a sincere faith. (v. 5)

Love. That's our target. That's what we're about—not championing political causes or impressing people. When we share what we know about Christ, people should sense that they're loved, not bullied.

---

4. A. Duane Litfin, "1 Timothy," in *The Bible Knowledge Commentary*, New Testament edition, ed. John F. Walvoord and Roy B. Zuck (Wheaton, Ill.: Scripture Press Publications, Victor Books, 1983), p. 731.

5. E. M. B. Green and C. J. Hemer, "Ephesus" in *The New Bible Dictionary*, 2d ed. (Downers Grove, Ill.: InterVarsity Press, 1982), p. 337.

And Christian love flows from (1) "a pure heart," where our "only desire is to help and to illumine and to lead nearer to God"[6]; (2) a "good conscience," where we are secure because we live up to what we teach; and (3) a "sincere faith," where we are earnest "in [our] desire to find the truth—and in [our] desire to communicate it."[7]

The false teachers, obviously, weren't aiming for the same goal. They were motivated by position and recognition. But Christians have a higher calling. Our goal is love.

Remember the Standard

Some of the false teachers even distorted God's Law in order to sway their audience.

> Some men, straying from these things, have turned aside to fruitless discussion, wanting to be teachers of the Law, even though they do not understand either what they are saying or the matters about which they make confident assertions. But we know that the Law is good, if one uses it lawfully, realizing the fact that law is not made for a righteous man, but for those who are lawless and rebellious, for the ungodly and sinners, for the unholy and profane, for those who kill their fathers or mothers, for murderers and immoral men and homosexuals and kidnappers and liars and perjurers, and whatever else is contrary to sound teaching. (vv. 6–10)

As one commentary explains, "The false teachers wanted to become famous as teachers of God's law, but they misunderstood the law's purpose. The law was not meant to give believers a list of commands for every occasion, but to show unbelievers their sin and bring them to God."[8] That's why Paul urged Timothy to remember

> sound teaching, according to the glorious gospel of the blessed God, with which I have been entrusted. (vv. 10b–11)

6. William Barclay, *The Letters to Timothy, Titus, and Philemon*, rev. ed., The Daily Study Bible Series (Philadelphia, Pa.: Westminster Press, 1975), p. 34.

7. Barclay, *Timothy, Titus, and Philemon*, p. 34.

8. Bruce B. Barton, David R. Veerman, Neil Wilson, *1 Timothy, 2 Timothy, Titus*, Life Application Bible Commentary Series (Wheaton, Ill.: Tyndale House Publishers, 1993), p. 26.

The gospel is our standard. Anything that distorts or denies salvation by grace is unsound doctrine. That's the message with which we've been entrusted, pastors and parishioners alike. When we tell others about our Lord Jesus, we need to ask ourselves if we're building the message from the foundation of the gospel.

Obey the Command

We'll look at Paul's testimony (vv. 12–17) in the next chapter. For now, let's take a look at Paul's fifth and last piece of advice to his friend.

> This command I entrust to you, Timothy, my son, in accordance with the prophecies previously made concerning you, that by them you may fight the good fight, keeping faith and a good conscience, which some have rejected and suffered shipwreck in regard to their faith. Among these are Hymenaeus and Alexander, whom I have delivered over to Satan, so that they may be taught not to blaspheme. (vv. 18–20)

What's the command? "Fight the good fight." We Christians are in a battle, even though we can't always see or feel it (see Eph. 6:12). And, as in any fight, we need weapons. In spiritual warfare, we're to wield "faith" and "a good conscience" (1 Tim. 1:19a; see also v. 5; 3:9). What happens if we leave these defenses locked in the armory? We could end up like Hymenaeus and Alexander (1:20), who suffered defeat and surrendered their faith to the enemy.

Wrap-up Warning to All Who Minister

The ministry, in particular the pastorate, can be the most disillusioning work in the world . . . or the most fulfilling. It all depends on whom we lean on and whom we listen to.

Those who lean on human opinion and listen to people more than they listen to God will have trouble. Their direction, vision, and philosophy will be shaped by those around them. They'll miss God's best and wind up disappointed, confused, and insecure.

For those who lean on the Lord and listen to His Word, the ministry will still be a challenge. But their direction, vision, and philosophy will be shaped by the Master. These people will serve Christ with fulfillment and enthusiasm.

Perhaps the want ad should read something like this:

> **Minister Wanted.** Prefer the compassion and care of a shepherd, the discipline and steadfastness of a warrior, and the zeal of a prophet. Main responsibilities: Love the truth; teach the truth; live the truth. Clay feet required—must be one of us.

 Living Insights

Can you spot false teaching? Could you explain the differences between Christianity and New Age philosophy? Or Mormonism? Or Jehovah's Witnesses? If someone from a cult came to your door, would you feel secure enough to dialogue with that person about Jesus Christ, the Bible, human sinfulness, and God's grace?

Like Timothy, we should know God's Word well enough to defend our faith when false doctrines cast a shadow of doubt over Christianity. Sadly, though, many Christians haven't taken the time to develop a solid understanding and defense of the Christian faith. They're stumped and silenced by such questions as "How do you know Jesus rose from the dead?" . . . "How do you know the Bible is the Word of God?" . . . and "Aren't there many ways to God?"

When it comes to solidifying our faith, nothing can take the place of diligent Bible study. Why not take some time to study the following passages and ground yourself in some of the doctrines of Christianity most assaulted by cults?

Humanity's inherent sinfulness: Psalm 51:5; Romans 3:9–18; 5:12; 7:20; Ephesians 2:1–3. - *you were dead in your transgressions & sins.*

Ps. 51:5 Surely I was sinful at birth, sinful from the time my mother conceived me.

Rom. 3:10 there is no one righteous, not even one. 5:12 sin entered thru one man, & death thru sin, & in this way death came to all men... 7:20 now if I do what I do not want to do, it is no longer I who do it, but it is sin living in me that does it.

Christ's substitutionary death: John 15:13; Romans 5:8; 2 Corinthians 5:21; Titus 2:13–14; 1 Peter 3:18.

Jn. 15:13 greater love has no one than this, that he lay down his life for his friends.

Rom. 5:8 But God demonstrates his own love for us in this: while we were still sinners, Christ died for us.

2 Cor. 5:21 God made him who had no sin to be sin for us, so that in him we might become the righteousness of God.

15

Titus 2:13-14 while we wait for the blessed hope --the glorious appearing of our great God & Savior, Jesus Christ, who gave himself for us to redeem us from all wickedness & to purify for himself a people that are his very own, eager to do what is good

1 Peter 3:18 for Christ died for sins once for all, the righteous for the unrighteous, to bring you to God. He was put to death in the body but made alive by the Spirit.

Salvation by faith, not works: John 3:1–16; Romans 3:21–28; Ephesians 2:8–10.

John 3:5 no one can enter the Kingdom of God unless he is born of water & the Spirit

Rom. 3:23 for all have sinned and fall short of the glory of God.

Eph. 2:8-10 for it is by grace you have been saved, through faith -- and this not from yourselves, it is the gift of God -- not by works, so that no one can boast. for we are God's workmanship, created in Christ Jesus to do good works, which

Deity of Christ: John 1:1, 14: *God prepared in advance for us to do.*

John 1:1 In the beginning was the Word, & the Word was w/ God, & the Word was God. v. 14 The Word became flesh & made his dwelling among us. We have seen his glory, the glory of the One & Only, who came from the Father, full of grace & truth.

Remember, no matter how much we learn, the riches of God's Word are never completely excavated. There's enough truth to keep us digging, and growing, for a lifetime.

Chapter 3

UNDESERVED MERCY FOR AN UNBELIEVING RABBI

1 Timothy 1:12–17

We now present one of those commercials whose message seems too good to be true . . .

A woman—mid-forties, bright smile, healthful glow—stands beside a swimming pool, holding out a pair of gigantic blue jeans. The denim curtain veils most of her body. Only her legs from the knees down and her neck and head are visible.

"These are the jeans I used to wear," she says, "before I lost two hundred pounds on the Suddenly Slim miracle diet. Now I use them to cover my swimming pool in the winter."

She tosses the jeans aside, revealing a svelte, bronze figure in a white bikini. "Thanks, Suddenly Slim. I couldn't have done it without you!"

---◆---

"Before and after" advertisements. We've all seen them. They hawk everything from diets to health-club memberships to toupees. And the testimonies are always the same. "I've never been happier." "My husband says I'm a different person." "People still notice me, but for all the right reasons." "The results are miraculous."

Such product-induced alterations, however, can hardly qualify as miracles. Impressive? Yes. Obvious? Of course. Long-term? Sometimes. But not miraculous. Only the supernatural touch of God can bring that kind of change—the kind that took place in the apostle Paul's life.

Paul: Before and After

Paul's life is the quintessential "before and after" story. Before his conversion, Saul of Tarsus was a meticulous observer of the Law—at least outwardly. A Pharisee among Pharisees, he was the cream of the crop. No doubt he saw himself as a paragon of piety and looked down on those who settled for less than perfection (look at Phil. 3:4–6). A gifted student, he sat under the tutelage of the distinguished teacher Gamaliel (Acts 22:3).

Saul's misguided zeal for the Law led him to hate Christians. He was present at the stoning of Stephen, then ruthlessly hunted down other followers of "The Way" (Acts 7:58–8:3). He tore them from their homes, threw them in prison, even approved of their torture and death. All the while, he considered his zealous persecution of Christians a service to God.

Then, on his way to Damascus, Saul ran head-on into the blinding grace of God (9:1–19a). The Lord Jesus Christ transformed him into a champion of the gospel, and he began to openly condemn the legalistic system he once followed. He preached that Christ alone makes people righteous. And the hatred for Jesus and His people that once darkened his heart gave way to unwavering love for both Savior and saints.

His former enemies were aghast at the change; many didn't trust him at first (v. 26). But the transformation was real. Eventually, Paul even gave his life for the movement he had once tried to extinguish. That's a miraculous change.

It amazed no one more than it did Paul. Whether speaking to allies or accusers, he used his testimony regularly as evidence of God's grace. His letters drip with gratitude for the Lord's mercy. And woven into his theology are reflections of God's loving intervention.

As Paul wrote to Timothy about the pure truth of the gospel, he couldn't help including how radically that message had affected his own life.

The Glorious Gospel

Having spent ten verses describing the primacy of sound teaching and the dangers of false doctrine (1 Tim. 1:1–10), Paul now reveals the basis for preaching the truth.

> According to the glorious gospel of the blessed God, with which I have been entrusted. (v. 11)

The gospel. That's where sound doctrine is rooted—in a message of grace, not works; in freedom, not bondage. Its origin is our blessed God Himself, who thought of it, implemented it through His Son, Jesus Christ, and empowered it through His Holy Spirit. And we have the joy and privilege of sharing the gospel treasure with others, as Paul did so many years ago.

The Thankful Apostle

What a thought! God's glittering gospel jewel entrusted to us. That spark of realization seems to touch off a flame of gratitude in Paul, leading him to praise and worship.

A Declaration of Gratitude

> I thank Christ Jesus our Lord, who has strengthened me, because He considered me faithful, putting me into service. (v. 12)

No wonder Paul exudes gratefulness! Just look at what Christ did for him. First, He gave Paul strength. Paul's energy and power for ministry came from Christ Himself. Not from a seminary education; not through church growth gimmicks; and not by personal charisma.

That's a reminder for us too. Ministry *for* Christ must be rooted *in* Christ. Without Him at the center of all we do, we're just playing at religion.

Second, Christ "considered [Paul] faithful"—He trusted him. William Barclay underscores the significance of such trust.

> Sometimes we forgive a man who has committed some mistake or been guilty of some sin, but we make it very clear that his past makes it impossible for us to trust him again with any responsibility. But Christ had not only forgiven Paul; he entrusted him with work to do. The man who had been Christ's persecutor had been made his ambassador.[1]

And third, Jesus put Paul "into service." Paul didn't sign himself up for the job of apostle; God selected him. And notice what Barclay observes: "It was for service, not honour, that Paul knew himself to be chosen."[2]

Paul never got over God's free gift of grace to a sinner like him.

An Admission of Guilt

Paul's background makes it clear that he wasn't chosen for his purity or obedience; he was chosen in spite of his lack of those qualities. In fact, Paul reveals

---

1. William Barclay, *The Letters to Timothy, Titus, and Philemon*, rev. ed., The Daily Study Bible Series (Philadelphia, Pa.: Westminster Press, 1975), p. 42.

2. Barclay, *The Letters to Timothy, Titus, and Philemon*, p. 42.

even though I was formerly a blasphemer and a persecutor and a violent aggressor. And yet I was shown mercy, because I acted ignorantly in unbelief. (v. 13)

Before Christ intervened in Paul's life, he was a blasphemer — an insulter of God. He was also a persecutor. As Barclay notes, Paul "had taken every means open to him under the Jewish law to annihilate the Christian Church."[3]

Not exactly a nice guy. But there's more. See the phrase *violent aggressor?* Barclay explains that the Greek word *hubristes*

> indicates a kind of arrogant sadism; it describes the man who is out to inflict pain for the sheer joy of inflicting it. . . .
>
> . . . Not content with words of insult, [Paul] went to the limit of legal persecution. Not content with legal persecution, he went to the limit of sadistic brutality in his attempt to stamp out the Christian faith.[4]

How could a guy like that end up in God's service? The same way we all do: by God's mercy. He chooses us, not on the basis of anything good in us, for "all our righteous deeds are like a filthy garment" (Isa. 64:6). Rather, He dispenses His mercy and grace to whomever He pleases. For Paul, the sweet aroma of mercy still lingers.

A Demonstration of Grace

Paul's life proves that no one's sin can outrun the loving pursuit of God's grace.

> And the grace of our Lord was more than abundant, with the faith and love which are found in Christ Jesus. (1 Tim. 1:14; also read Rom. 5:20)

God's grace, received by faith in Jesus Christ, was more than sufficient to cover and cleanse Paul's sin.

How about you? Do you ever wonder if you've committed a sin too heinous for God to forgive? Impossible. The shadow of sin, though sometimes long, broad, and dark, can never obscure the light of God's grace. He died for *all* our sins—big ones, small ones,

---

3. Barclay, *The Letters to Timothy, Titus, and Philemon,* p. 45.

4. Barclay, *The Letters to Timothy, Titus, and Philemon,* pp. 45–46.

private ones, public ones. The ones we struggle with, and the ones we're not even aware of. Once we put our trust in Christ, we stand under the endless fountain of His precious blood, which cleanses every sin we ever committed or will commit.

Hang on. There's more.

> It is a trustworthy statement, deserving full acceptance, that Christ Jesus came into the world to save sinners, among whom I am foremost of all. And yet for this reason I found mercy, in order that in me as the foremost, Jesus Christ might demonstrate His perfect patience, as an example for those who would believe in Him for eternal life. (vv. 15–16)

Paul puts the gospel in a nutshell: "Jesus came to save sinners," he says, "and if He can save *me*, He can save anybody." The foremost of sinners? Paul? We never think of him that way, do we? We use words like "supersaint" and "apostle." Not the foremost of sinners. But that's how he saw himself. And that's why God's grace meant so much to him (see also 1 Cor. 15:9; Eph. 3:8).

See the word *example* (1 Tim. 1:16)? In Greek, it's the word *hupotuposis*, which means "an outline, a sketch-plan, a first draft, a preliminary model."[5] We might call it a prototype. That's how Paul saw himself—a model with a sign hanging on it that read, "This is what a life looks like when it's shaped by the grace of God . . . and it could be your life."

Do you know that God is working in you so that others can see His handiwork? So let His grace shine through. You never know who might be watching.

The Worthy King

The hallmark of Paul's experience with God can be summed up in one word—*mercy* (vv. 13, 16). Someone has said that mercy is God's ministry to the miserable. So it is. And how should formerly miserable saints respond to God's mercy? How else but with praise to our Almighty King:

> Now to the King eternal, immortal, invisible, the only God, be honor and glory forever and ever. Amen. (v. 17)

5. Barclay, *The Letters to Timothy, Titus, and Philemon*, p. 48.

21

God deserves the glory for Paul's "before and after" story . . . and ours too.

 Living Insights

When was the last time you reflected on your own "before and after" story? Have you thought much about where you came from and where you are now? Why not take some time to reflect on the changes God has wrought in your life? Using the space provided, explore the differences in your attitudes and actions before you knew Christ as your Savior and now.

My Life before Christ   **My Life with Christ**

_____   _____

_____   _____

_____   _____

_____   _____

_____   _____

_____   _____

_____   _____

_____   _____

Now, use this record of God's mercy and grace as fuel for the fires of worship. Feel free to read verse 17 aloud as part of your response, or write down your own thoughts as they come to mind.

_____

_____

_____

_____

_____

Amazing, isn't it? You might even say . . . miraculous.

Chapter 4

WHAT'S *FIRST* IN A MEANINGFUL MINISTRY?

1 Timothy 2:1–4, 8

Ministry.

Quick! What comes to mind when you see that word? The pastor's desk, buried under a heap of phone messages, books, and doughnut crumbs?

Maybe a collage of images flashes across your mind. The pastor running to his car, sport coat half on, already late for the next appointment. Panic-stricken teachers throwing together a Sunday school lesson Saturday at midnight. The choir rehearsing the Christmas musical—arguing over whose child will play the baby Jesus and who will sing the solo.

Pastors too exhausted to pastor. Schedules crammed full of church events. Saints stretched to the limit. And no rest in sight.

Does busyness make a meaningful ministry? Is God pleased when we kick up so much dust and debris? Eugene Peterson doesn't think so. He writes,

> Hilary of Tours diagnosed our pastoral busyness as *irreligiosa sollicitudo pro Deo,* a blasphemous anxiety to do God's work for him.[1]

Ouch! The truth hurts. Most Christian workers, especially pastors, are just too busy. Why? Peterson gives two reasons. One,

> *I am busy because I am vain.* I want to appear important. Significant. What better way than to be busy? The incredible hours, the crowded schedule, and the heavy demands on my time are proof to myself— and to all who will notice—that I am important.[2]

---

1. Eugene Peterson, *The Contemplative Pastor: Returning to the Art of Spiritual Direction* (Grand Rapids, Mich.: William B. Eerdmans Publishing Co., 1989), pp. 17–18.

2. Peterson, *The Contemplative Pastor,* p. 18.

And two,

> *I am busy because I am lazy.* I indolently let others decide what I will do instead of resolutely deciding myself. . . .
>
> It was a favorite theme of C. S. Lewis that only lazy people work hard. By lazily abdicating the essential work of deciding and directing, establishing values and setting goals, other people do it for us; then we find ourselves frantically, at the last minute, trying to satisfy a half dozen different demands on our time, none of which is essential to our vocation, to stave off the disaster of disappointing someone.[3]

What, then, is first on Peterson's list of pastoral priorities? Prayer.

> I want to do the original work of being in deepening conversation with the God who reveals himself to me and addresses me by name. I don't want to dispense mimeographed hand-outs that describe God's business; I want to witness out of my own experience. I don't want to live as a parasite on the first-hand spiritual life of others, but to be personally involved with all my senses, tasting and seeing that the Lord is good.[4]

He's not alone. In 1 Timothy 2, Paul exhorts Timothy to put prayer at the top of his priority list. So let's slow down the pace, allow the dust to settle, and learn how to regain the preeminence of prayer.

The Biblical Perspective on Prayer

Let's start by doing a little investigating. Is it accurate to say that prayer should be the top priority in ministry? Does the New Testament present prayer with such urgency? We only need to glance at a few passages for the answer.

- Read Acts 6:1–4. "We will devote ourselves to prayer, and to the ministry of the word," the apostles said. Of these two primary ministries, prayer came first. So they found a way to maintain

---

3. Peterson, *The Contemplative Pastor*, pp. 18–19.

4. Peterson, *The Contemplative Pastor*, pp. 19–20.

24

their top priorities and still meet the physical needs of an expanding church.

- Read Ephesians 6:13–19. "Pray at all times," with alertness and perseverance "for all the saints," Paul exhorts. Prayer is an indispensable weapon in our battle against Satan and his forces.

- Read Hebrews 4:15–16. "Draw near with *confidence* to the throne of grace," the writer urges. Jesus, our Great Intercessor, sympathizes with all our weaknesses. And He wants us to come to Him as our first recourse, not our last, so He can help us with His abundant mercy and grace.

- Read James 4:2. "You do not have," James bluntly states, "because you do not ask." He admonished his readers for not approaching God with their needs.

- Read Philippians 4:6–7. "Be anxious for nothing," but tell God your requests and let Him guard you with His peace. According to Paul, prayer is the best way to stop worrying.

Are you overwhelmed by ministry demands? Pray. Are you under spiritual attack? Pray. Is temptation about to get the best of you? Pray. Are you lacking? Are you anxious? Pray, pray, pray.

Does that mean we never seek counsel from friends or that we forsake Bible study to log more prayer time? Of course not. But prayer should flow through every situation, reminding us that everything we do depends on our Father in heaven.

Common Distortions of Prayer

Prayer, though, just like any spiritual activity, can be misused, distorted, or relegated to a mechanical regimen. So before looking at Paul's instructions to Timothy, let's examine some common ways we diminish prayer's effectiveness.

Hypocrisy: Turning Prayer into a Public Performance

Jesus attacked this practice when He exposed the public prayers of the Pharisees as shallow displays of piety meant solely to impress other people (Matt. 6:5–8). Our Father, who knows our every need, is to be our focus; not people.

Formality: Limiting Prayer to a Specific Time and Place

Prayer shouldn't be limited by time and location. This doesn't mean we should surrender that reflective prayer by the bedside at night. It simply means that God hears us, no matter the hour or place. Paul told the Thessalonians, "Pray without ceasing" (1 Thess. 5:17). Communing with God throughout the day, anytime, anywhere, expresses our complete dependence on Him.

Passivity: Using Prayer as a Substitute for Action

George Buttrick rightly observed, "Prayer is not a substitute for work, thinking, watching, suffering, or giving; prayer is a support for all other efforts."[5]

Some things don't require prayer for a decision. For example, we don't need to pray about whether to reconcile with an offended brother or sister. We need to stop what we're doing—even if it's worship—and go to that person (Matt. 5:23–24). We don't need to pray about whether we should share the gospel, study the Word, love our spouses, or worship in a local church. These are all commanded in Scripture. When we know what we ought to be doing, we need to do it, not use prayer as an excuse to avoid it.

Emergency: Making Prayer a Last Resort

Flare prayers. We've all used them. We're cruising along, convinced that we're in control. Then darkness closes in, and we start to drift into danger. "Where is God?" we wonder. So we grab our flare gun and fire off a round or two toward heaven, hoping God will see the flash and come to the rescue. "When all else fails, pray" isn't exactly what God has in mind. He wants us to come to Him all the time, not just when we're in trouble.

God's Directives regarding Prayer

We've covered the mandate to pray and the wrong ways to pray. Now let's delve into 1 Timothy 2 and discover how to pray God's way.

What Are We to Do?

> First of all, then, I urge that entreaties and prayers, petitions and thanksgivings, be made on behalf of all men. (1 Tim. 2:1)

Notice that we're to make prayer primary in ministry. "First of

---

5. George Buttrick, as quoted in *Quote, Unquote*, comp. Lloyd Cory (Wheaton, Ill.: Scripture Press Publications, Victor Books, 1977), p. 247.

all, then, I urge," Paul says (v. 1a). He seems to be acknowledging that Timothy's ministry platter is full and that something has to come first—a non-negotiable, a must. That's prayer, according to Paul. He doesn't merely suggest it as a good idea. He urges his friend to give prayer the attention it deserves.

What shape, then, should prayer take? What should the activity of prayer look like? Paul uses four terms to describe different aspects of prayer, each one is important—*entreaties*, *prayers*, *petitions*, and *thanksgivings*.

Entreaties. The fundamental idea behind the Greek word for *entreaty* is a request made to satisfy a need. This is the starting point for prayer. As William Barclay says, prayer "begins with the conviction that we cannot deal with life ourselves. That sense of human weakness is the basis of all approach to God."[6]

Prayers. The word for *prayers* emphasizes the person of God. The New Testament usage signifies "something very personal and specific, a genuine conversation with God or Jesus Christ."[7] In using this word, Paul reminds Timothy that our prayers amount to more than wishful thinking. They allow us to converse with the God of the universe, the One who supplies all of our needs, great and small. And that allows for a changed perspective on God's power and our problems.

Petitions. This word pictures someone entering a king's presence to submit an official request. "That tells us much about prayer," says Barclay. "It tells us that the way to God stands open and that we have the right to bring our petitions to one who is a king."[8]

Thanksgivings. An important ingredient in all our prayers ought to be *thanksgivings*. We should be as ready to thank God for His provisions as we are to ask for them. Do we focus more on grumbling and complaining and "telling God on" someone than on being grateful for all that we have? There's no better place than prayer to cultivate a thankful attitude.

Prayer, then, involves coming to God with all our needs—spiritual and physical—and thanking Him for all the ways He meets them.

---

6. William Barclay, *The Letters to Timothy, Titus, and Philemon*, rev. ed., The Daily Study Bible Series (Philadelphia, Pa.: Westminster Press, 1975), p. 57.

7. Hans Schönweiss, "Prayer," in *The New International Dictionary of New Testament Theology*, ed. Colin Brown (Grand Rapids, Mich.: Zondervan Publishing House, Regency Reference Library, 1986), vol. 2, p. 867.

8. Barclay, *The Letters to Timothy, Titus, and Philemon*, p. 58.

For Whom Are We to Pray?

Should we offer prayer only for those in the body of Christ? Not according to Paul, who says we should pray

> on behalf of all men, for kings and all who are in authority. (vv. 1b–2a)

One wonders how Timothy might have responded to Paul's command. "Pray for Nero? That Christian-killing maniac?" That's right. There's no qualifier in the text. *All* who are in authority— whether they abuse that authority or recognize it as God-given.

What would happen if we prayed for those in authority as often as we criticized them? Members of the school board. The mayor. Judges. Councilmen and councilwomen. The governor. Those who fill the seats of the House of Representatives and the Senate. All the way up to the president. Remember, God has given those in authority the ability to influence society. And our prayers can have an influence on them. Which brings us to our reason for praying.

Why Are We to Pray?

Our prayer for those in authority has a purpose:

> in order that we may lead a tranquil and quiet life in all godliness and dignity. This is good and acceptable in the sight of God our Savior, who desires all men to be saved and to come to the knowledge of the truth. (vv. 2b–4)

Notice the dual purpose. First, prayer can influence authorities to foster an environment that allows Christians to live in peace— which leads to the second, ultimate, purpose of spreading the gospel.

So pray for our leaders, whether they're Christians or not. Pray that they come to faith in Christ. Pray that their decisions honor God and allow for the free spread of the gospel. Pray that God would reach into the souls of our local, state, national, and world leaders who don't know Him. That He would save them, and incline their wills toward His. Our prayers can make a difference.

How Are We to Pray?

You knew we would get to the practicalities, right? What form should prayer take? Is body position important? What about time, location, frequency, and duration? Let's drop down to verse 8.

Therefore I want the men in every place to pray,
lifting up holy hands, without wrath and dissension.

"In every place" encourages us to pray outside the church walls.
We don't have to wait for that sacred spot, the proper time during
the service, or until life "gets back to normal." Pray in the car or
while doing the laundry. Pray when you're up or down. Early or
late. In the heat of stress or the cool breeze of leisure. Pray in any
place, at any time. God's ears are always open.

"Lifting up holy hands" has more to do with spiritual condition
than body position. In New Testament times, the lifting of the
hands in prayer signified internal cleanness. Philip Towner eluci-
dates Paul's meaning here.

> The early church understood such purity to be a
> condition of acceptable prayer (Jas. 4:8). When we
> pray, our communication is with a holy God. He
> requires of us that we deal with our sins before mak-
> ing our approach.[9]

We should approach God in purity. That means not only confessing our sins to Him but maintaining pure relationships with
others. Simmering anger, bitterness, hatred, division, gossip—these
have no place in a Christian relationship. In fact, disharmony with
others can hinder our prayer life (see 1 Pet. 3:7).

Practical Suggestions for Making Prayer a Priority

So what can we do, practically speaking, to give prayer the
prominent place it deserves? Here are three thoughts.

First, *form a habit*. If we don't plan to pray, chances are we won't.
Of course, prayer can erupt spontaneously. But regular times of
undisturbed prayer will keep us deliberately focused on our Father.

Second, *set no limit*. Pray about everything, no matter how confident you feel about a decision or how routine an activity or event
seems. We need God's strength for all of life, not just the "biggies."

Third, *restrain all substitutes*. Don't let anything take the place
of prayer. Books are helpful. The counsel of friends is needed. But
don't let those nudge prayer out of the top spot. Of all the spiritual
resources available to us, what could be more effective than direct

9. Philip H. Towner, *1–2 Timothy and Titus* (Downers Grove, Ill.: InterVarsity Press, 1994),
p. 70.

conversation with the King of the universe?

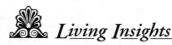 *Living Insights*

Prayer can be a struggle . . . and often should be. For, as John Henry Jowett once wrote,

> It is in the field of prayer that life's critical battles are lost or won. . . . In prayer we bring our spiritual enemies into the Presence of God and we fight them there.[10]

Sometimes, though, we struggle in prayer because we let our emotions or preconceptions about God distort our image of Him. We wonder if He can really hear us. Or if He hears us, we doubt that He cares enough to listen. Sometimes we have no trouble seeing Him as an all-powerful King. But we can't imagine Him as an attentive Father. Jowett reminds us that, regardless of how we feel, our prayers are heard by a Father who loves His children.

> I am coming to a King, but I am coming to more than a King. I am coming to a Father, and Father-hood is larger than Kingship, just as home is larger than a throne. A king may have gifts at his disposal and may have honors and benefits and offices to confer upon his subjects, but fatherhood moves in a circle of intimacies and shared secrets, even in the matchless commerce of truth and grace and love. When prayer turns into this marvellous realm it is not so much a suppliant, laden with petition, as a wondering child walking in the revealing companionship of the Father in heaven. Prayer is not always like Lazarus, clothed in rags and bowing in suppliancy at the rich man's gate; it is sometimes like Lazarus in the Father's bosom, resting in the secret place of the Most High, and walking and talking in the shadow of the Almighty.[11]

10. John Henry Jowett, "Where Our Greatest Battles Are Fought," in *Classic Sermons on Prayer*, comp. Warren W. Wiersbe (Grand Rapids, Mich.: Kregel Publications, 1987), p. 56.

11. Jowett, "Where Our Greatest Battles Are Fought," p. 53.

When you approach God in prayer, do you feel that you're coming to a loving Father? Why or why not?

_____

_____

_____

What are the main struggles you face when it comes to prayer?

_____

_____

_____

Do you believe that your heavenly Father wants to help you overcome these struggles? How do you think He might do that?

_____

_____

_____

Chapter 5

GOD'S DESIRE, MAN'S DEBT, CHRIST'S PAYMENT

1 Timothy 2:3–7

People don't always get along. Labor and management get hung up in contract settlements. Professional athletes go toe-to-toe with team owners. And truck drivers haggle with those who use their services.

That's why we need mediators. They negotiate terms beneficial to both sides, helping bridge gaps and mend rifts between two opposing parties.

For example, have you ever been to court? Then you've probably used a mediator—a judge who heard both sides of the argument and rendered a fair decision. And if you've ever stepped between two children fighting over a toy, you know firsthand what it's like to serve as a mediator!

What's So Important about a Mediator?

Eternally speaking, we would be lost without a mediator. If we need someone to arbitrate the conflicts of people, how much more do we need someone to make peace between sinful humanity and a holy God? Ever since Adam and Eve brought sin into the world, no one has been able to stand before God without a mediator to plead his or her case.

In Scripture, we find a great illustration of mediation in the account of Job.

The Case of Job

This Old Testament saint had lost everything—his children, his possessions, even his health. Why would God allow such catastrophes to overwhelm one who loved Him so faithfully? Well-meaning friends, like Bildad the Shuhite, offered explanations for Job's predicament.

> "Does God pervert justice
> Or does the Almighty pervert what is right?
> If your sons sinned against Him,

Then He delivered them into the power of their
   transgression." (Job 8:3-4)

In other words, "You're in sin, Job; that's why you're suffering."
But Job wants to take his case before God. He knows, however,
that Bildad is at least half right. Job, like every human being, is a
sinner. And how can a sinner argue with God?

Then Job answered,
"In truth I know that this is so,
But how can a man be in the right before God?
If one wished to dispute with Him,
He could not answer Him once in a thousand times.
Wise in heart and mighty in strength,
Who has defied Him without harm?" (Job 9:1-4)

Our gaping, ragged righteousness can't compare with the perfect
completeness of God's holiness. We can't treat Him as a peer, Job
continues:

"For He is not a man as I am that I may answer
   Him,
That we may go to court together." (v. 32)

Job, in his great need, wished for a mediator.

"There is no umpire between us,
Who may lay his hand upon us both." (v. 33)

The Role of Priests

To help span the chasm between Himself and humanity, God
instituted the priesthood. The Old Testament priests and the sacrifices they administered provided a way for God's people to walk
with Him, even though they sinned. Hebrews 5:1-3 beautifully
describes the role of the priestly "umpire."

For every high priest taken from among men is
appointed on behalf of men in things pertaining to
God, in order to offer both gifts and sacrifices for
sins; he can deal gently with the ignorant and misguided, since he himself also is beset with weakness;
and because of it he is obligated to offer sacrifices
for sins, as for the people, so also for himself.

Though they were designated as mediators, the priests still weren't perfect. So God gave us the perfect Mediator in Jesus Christ.

> Since then we have a great high priest who has passed through the heavens, Jesus the Son of God, let us hold fast our confession. For we do not have a high priest who cannot sympathize with our weaknesses, but one who has been tempted in all things as we are, yet without sin. Let us therefore draw near with confidence to the throne of grace, that we may receive mercy and may find grace to help in time of need. (Heb. 4:14–16)

Christ our Mediator has built a bridge between us and God. Two parties, once infinitely distant, have been brought intimately close.

How Does Mediation Relate to the Gospel?

Jesus Christ as Mediator figures prominently in Paul's theology and presentation of the gospel (read Rom. 5:1; 2 Cor. 5:18–21; Eph. 2:13; Col. 1:19–23). And his letter to Timothy is no exception. In 1 Timothy 2:1–7, Christ's mediation on our behalf is the fuel that fires Paul's exhortation to pray.

The Context: Prayer

As we learned in the previous chapter, Paul wants Timothy to make prayer a primary and pervasive activity. He urges Timothy to pray for all people (v. 1), especially for those in authority (v. 2).

The Motive: Salvation

Why pray for everyone? So that Christians "may lead a tranquil and quiet life in all godliness and dignity" (v. 2b). But that's only the immediate motive. Ultimately, God wants us to pray because He has established prayer as part of the process of salvation.

> This is good and acceptable in the sight of God our Savior, who desires all men[1] to be saved and to come to the knowledge of the truth. (vv. 3–4)

---

1. The Greek word Paul uses here is *anthropos*, which refers generally to "mankind" rather than specifically to the male gender. It's also used in vv. 4 and 5. We get our word *anthropology* from it.

God desires[2] the salvation of all people (note the repeated emphasis of the word *all* in verses 1, 2, 4, 6). As Christians, His desires become our desires. So we pray for all people to be saved.

In 1 Cor. 9:19, Paul demonstrates the lengths to which we should go to reflect this desire to a lost world.

> For though I am free from all men, I have made
> myself a slave to all, that I might win the more.

Paul's concern is for all humanity, even though he realizes only some will be saved (1 Cor. 9:22b; see also 2 Pet. 3:9). The offer of salvation is universal, though not all will take it.

The Doctrine: Ransom

Now Paul explains one of the greatest of all doctrinal truths: how God saves sinners.

> For there is one God, and one mediator also between
> God and men, the man Christ Jesus. (1 Tim. 2:5)

First, he says there is "one God." This truth alone (monotheism) distinguished Christianity from the cultural religion of the Roman world, which promoted the worship of multiple gods (pantheism).

There's one God—holy, pure, perfect. So how can we, as sinners, relate to Him? Through a mediator, the *only* mediator between God and humankind—Jesus Christ. As both undiminished deity and true humanity, Jesus alone could bridge the separation between us and the God of the universe.

How did He build that bridge? Verse 6 tells us He

> gave Himself as a ransom for all, the testimony borne
> at the proper time.

The Greek work for *ransom, antilutron,* depicts

> the exchange price for freeing a slave or redeeming
> a prisoner of war. It illustrates that Christ exchanged

---

2. Commentator Ernest R. Campbell illuminates the meaning of the word *desires* for us: "It is important to observe the overwhelming common meaning of this word, namely, *wish*. . . . This predominant meaning is *totally void* of the idea of determination or fixity. The basic meaning floats in the area of something a person *would like to see happen*. . . . Paul is declaring that God *desires, wants, wishes,* and *longs* for all men to be saved. It is an expression of the *sympathetic heart of God* compassionately reaching out to all." *First Timothy* (Silverton, Oreg.: Canyonview Press, 1983), p. 73.

his life for ours.[3]

Here's how this all ties together: For the holy and pure God to come together with sinful humanity, a bridge had to be built. Jesus Christ, the God-man, is that bridge. By paying sin's penalty in our stead—which meant giving His life—Jesus enables us to cross the bridge of His sacrifice and walk into our Father's loving embrace (see also Matt. 20:28; Mark 10:45).

As Major W. Ian Thomas summed up, "If the life that Christ lived qualified Him for the death that He died, then the death that He died qualifies you for the life that He lived!"[4] The gospel is indeed *good news!*

Paul's Purpose: Proclamation

Christ's mediation on our behalf, however, is more than a fact to be understood. It's a message that must be communicated. Paul's ministry was driven by his passion to share that message. In fact, God *appointed* him to three roles, all of which were designed to spread the gospel.

> And for this I was appointed a *preacher* and an *apostle* (I am telling the truth, I am not lying) as a *teacher* of the Gentiles in faith and truth. (1 Tim. 2:7, emphasis added)

First, God appointed Paul as a preacher, which William Barclay defines as

> a *herald* of the story of Jesus Christ. A herald is a man who makes a statement and who says: "This is true." He is a man who brings a proclamation that is not his own, but which comes from the king.[5]

Paul was God's mouthpiece—an announcer for the King's good news.

God also bestowed the office of apostle on Paul. The word *apostle*

---

3. Bruce B. Barton, David R. Veerman, Neil Wilson, *1 Timothy, 2 Timothy, Titus*, Life Application Bible Commentary Series (Wheaton, Ill.: Tyndale House Publishers, 1993), p. 44.

4. Major W. Ian Thomas, *The Mystery of Godliness* (Grand Rapids, Mich.: Zondervan Publishing House, 1964), p. 132.

5. William Barclay, *The Letters to Timothy, Titus, and Philemon*, rev. ed., The Daily Study Bible Series (Philadelphia, Pa.: Westminster Press, 1975), p. 63.

literally means "one sent forth."[6] In secular Greek, it carried the thought of an official envoy or divinely sent teacher.[7] Paul was an official representative of Christ, commissioned to take His message throughout the world.

Finally, Paul was appointed a *teacher* to the Gentiles. Though teaching and preaching both focus on the gospel, the activities vary. Paul uses *preaching* primarily to describe the initial delivery of the gospel message (see Rom. 15:20; 1 Cor. 1:17; 2 Cor. 10:16; Gal. 1:8). *Teaching*, on the other hand, refers to deepening others in Christian doctrine (see 1 Tim. 1:3; 3:2; 4:11). Preaching is the declaration of truth directed at the will. Teaching is the explanation of truth directed at the mind. Both, however, have as their goal a changed life.

Paul's mention of the Gentiles here (2:7b) suggests that a significant focus of his ministry was to Gentiles. Grounding the Gentiles in the Scriptures was especially important because the Gentiles, unlike the Jews, had little or no exposure to the Old Testament and the promise of a coming Messiah.

Why Do We Value These Truths?

These truths Paul has communicated are valuable to us for at least three reasons.

First, they reveal the heart of God. God is not some cruel, distant despot. He's loving and compassionate. Why else would He have so radically expended Himself to provide a way for us to come to Him?

Second, they announce the plan of salvation. Packed into this small chunk of Scripture (1 Tim. 2:5–6) we find the infinite wonder of the gospel message. One God—pure, holy, perfect. All of humanity—sinful, rebellious, distant from God. One Mediator, Jesus Christ—the God-man whose perfect sacrifice built a bridge between us and God.

Third, they verify the validity of world evangelism and missions. The repetitive use of the world *all* (vv. 1, 2, 4, 6) and Paul's ministry to the Gentiles (v. 7) remind us that the gospel is for the entire world. That gets us beyond our neighborhood and our nation. God's message of

6. W. E. Vine, *Vine's Expository Dictionary of New Testament Words* (n.p., n.d.), p. 63.

7. Gerhard Kittel and Gerhard Friedrich, eds., *Theological Dictionary of the New Testament*, translated and abridged in one volume by Geoffrey W. Bromiley (1985; reprint, Grand Rapids, Mich.: William B. Eerdmans Publishing Co.; Devon, United Kingdom: Paternoster Press, 1988), pp. 67–68.

freedom is for everyone.

Thank God we have a Mediator and an Advocate. And a Bridge . . . that will never burn.

 Living Insights

Suppose two friends of yours weren't getting along. What would you be willing to do to reconcile them with one another? Would you meet them for lunch, perhaps, and help them work things out? Would you miss work? Would you chance losing one or both of them as a friend? Would you risk your own physical or emotional health? Would you . . . die for them? Probably not.

Now imagine that you're God. Perfect, all-powerful, infinite in knowledge and wisdom. Would you leave heaven and live on the earth you created? Would you take on the form of a man—a poor man? Then, would you willingly die so that the very people who would crucify you might be saved from eternal punishment and reconciled to you?

That's what Jesus did.

Christ's role as Mediator, though, didn't end with His death on the cross. He rose from the dead, ascended into heaven, and took His place at the right hand of God the Father. From there He renders our prayers acceptable to the Father, exercises His leadership over the church, and guides us along the road to spiritual maturity.

What does Christ's willingness to serve as Mediator tell you about:

• God's love for you and His desire to have fellowship with you?

_____

_____

_____

• God's commitment to hearing your prayers?

_____

_____

_____

- The necessity of depending on Christ Himself for your spiritual growth?

_____

_____

_____

> "Greater love has no one than this, that one lay down his life for his friends." (John 15:13)

No greater love indeed.

Chapter 6

WHAT ABOUT WOMEN IN THE CHURCH?

1 Timothy 2:9–15

How sweet are Thy words to my taste!
Yes, sweeter than honey to my mouth!
(Psalm 119:103)

The Word of God is sweet indeed. And nourishing too. But scooping a handful of honey can be dangerous . . . if you have to go through bees to get it.

Whenever a pastor dips his hand into the sticky topic of women's roles in the church, he invariably stirs up a bee's nest of controversy. And the loudest buzzes tend to come from two extreme positions.

One end of the spectrum labels as sexist any attempt to differentiate between the roles of men and women. People who hold this view promote a doctrine of sameness, in which women should be allowed to exercise the exact authority as men—as elders, pastors, and bishops. Any perspective that even suggests gender-based role distinctions is viewed with suspicion.

At the other end of the spectrum, role distinctions are a license to dominate women rather than encourage them to use their God-given gifts and abilities. The ideal woman, then, is a mousy creature who should be seen and not heard. Those who hold this view label as pro-feminist anyone who attempts to elevate the fairer sex.

As you might suspect, the balanced, biblical view lies somewhere between these two extremes. God's Word prescribes role distinctions while also preserving the equal dignity, worth, and spirituality of both sexes. So let's open the Word to 1 Timothy chapter 2 and take a taste of this topic. Oh, and keep your eyes open for bees.

What about Today's Woman?

A few observations about women in today's world will provide a starting point of comparison for our study.

First, in the world arena, *women have become more liberated than restrained.* Many doors once closed to women have been opened. Women can be doctors, lawyers, CEOs—even Supreme Court justices. Today's woman has many more choices open to her than her counterpart of thirty years ago.

Second, regarding home life, *women have become more assaulted than supported*. The extremely significant work of creating a caring, nurturing, life-enriching environment for the family—as well as the vital task of shaping children's lives—has been devalued in our society. The title "homemaker" produces smirks and put-downs today. One writer observes that women

> have been brainwashed to believe that the absence of a titled, payroll occupation enslaves a woman to failure, boredom, and imprisonment within the confines of home.[1]

Third, on the job, *women have become more respected than exploited*. Laws against sexual discrimination and harassment protect women's opportunities for success in today's business world. Also, women have steadily gained respect as able managers and administrators over the past two decades.

Fourth, as a result of these changing cultural trends and attitudes, *women in the church are more confused than informed*. Some tell women, "You can do anything a man can do," but others say, "You can't do anything in the church," leaving many Christian women frustrated, confused, unappreciated, or overworked. That's why we need to listen to the only absolutely reliable voice for a solution—the Word of God.

Several Key Passages

What does the Bible teach about the role of women in the church? We can't provide an exhaustive answer to that question in one study guide chapter, so let us first give you a list of key passages to consider on this subject.

Though we'll be referring to some of these passages in this study, you should spend some time working through them on your own. These, along with this lesson in 1 Timothy 2, will help you establish an informed position on women in the church.

Genesis 1–3   Galatians 3:28

1. Dorothy Patterson, "The High Calling of Wife and Mother in Biblical Perspective," in *Recovering Biblical Manhood and Womanhood: A Response to Evangelical Feminism*, ed. John Piper and Wayne Grudem (Wheaton, Ill.: Good News Publishers, Crossway Books, 1991), p. 365.

Judges 4:4–16   Ephesians 5:21–33
Acts 21:8–9   Colossians 3:18–19
1 Corinthians 11:1–16 Titus 2:3–5
1 Corinthians 14:34–36 1 Peter 3:1–7

One Crucial Paragraph: 1 Timothy 2:9–15

With all of this ground now covered, let's dive into our 1 Timothy passage. As always, the context gives us our bearings. Keep in mind that this epistle deals with *conduct within the church* (see 3:15), not society at large. In chapter 2, Paul has been addressing prayer (vv. 1–8). He tells Timothy to pray for "all men" (v. 1), because God desires "all men" to be saved (v. 4). The Greek word for *men* here is *anthropos*, the generic term for all of humanity. In verse 8, however, Paul switches terms:

> Therefore I want the men (*aner*) in every place to pray, lifting up holy hands, without wrath and dissension.

The word he uses here specifically denotes the male gender. Starting with verse 8, then, Paul begins to assign certain activities for both sexes. First and foremost, men are to turn away from anger and factious disputes and pray instead.

Paul isn't discouraging women from praying. In fact, he encourages all believers, including women, to pray in his other letters (see 1 Cor. 11:13; Phil. 4:6–7; Col. 4:2; 1 Thess. 5:17).

Rather, he's urging men to take the lead in the church. "If I come to Ephesus," we might paraphrase Paul, "I want to see the men coming to God in pure and unified prayer." Perhaps the men in the Ephesian church were neglecting their spiritual duties or quarreling. Or possibly some of the women were usurping male authority. Whatever the case, Paul clearly designates prayer as a priority for the men.

What Is Expected of Women?

Now he turns his attention to the women.

> Likewise, I want women to adorn themselves with proper clothing, modestly and discreetly, not with braided hair and gold or pearls or costly garments; but rather by means of good works, as befits women making a claim to godliness. (1 Tim. 2:9–10)

42

Likewise signals a connection with the previous verse. "Since men are to pray," Paul transitions, "what are the women to do?" First, they should dress properly, modestly, and discreetly (v. 9). Is that the extent of Paul's concern for women—how they dress? Not at all. Philip Towner explains that in Paul's culture, as in ours, wardrobe can affect worship.

> [Paul] prescribes a manner of dress with three very similar terms stressing modesty and discretion (NIV *modestly, with decency and propriety*). Some commentators suggest that the tone of this instruction is "sexual," Paul's intention being to discourage women from dressing in a way that would distract men in the worship service. But perhaps the more acute problem was that of insensitive women flaunting their dress, jewelry and hairstyles in a way that hurt the feelings of the poor and disturbed the church.[2]

Paul isn't discouraging tasteful makeup, attractive jewelry, and nicely-arranged fashions and accessories. His concern is that glitter and gaudiness not replace godliness. Character, not clothes, makes the woman.

And what better place to display godly character than in the worship service?

> Let a woman quietly receive instruction with entire submissiveness. But I do not allow a woman to teach or exercise authority over a man, but to remain quiet. (vv. 11–12)

Three imperatives for the godly behavior of women in church emerge from these verses. First, *a woman is to remain quiet rather than vocal* (v. 11a). Now, before we accuse Paul of sexism or downright meanness, let's get the full meaning from his words.

To begin with, Judaism discouraged women from learning *at all*. So Paul's instructions on *how* women should learn represent a philosophical shift from the exclusiveness of Judaism to the inclusiveness of Christianity.[3]

2. Philip H. Towner, *1–2 Timothy and Titus*, The IVP New Testament Commentary Series (Downers Grove, Ill.: InterVarsity Press, 1994), p. 71.

3. Douglas Moo, "What Does It Mean Not to Teach or Have Authority Over Men?" in *Recovering Biblical Manhood and Womanhood*, p. 183.

With that in mind, then, what does it mean for a woman to learn "quietly"? This verse is no gag rule for women to observe the moment they walk into the building. Rather, in the preaching service women should focus on listening instead of preaching. There's no reason to draw from this passage a contemporary prohibition against women singing in the service, teaching Sunday school, or performing a variety of other ministries.

Second, *a woman is to receive instruction rather than give instruction* (v. 11b). She is to learn with "entire submissiveness." We often recoil when we hear the word *submit* because it has been grossly misrepresented. The Greek word has no trace of imagery that suggests bowing down to men or allowing men to use women as doormats. As one commentary states,

> "Submission" doesn't imply that women surrender their mind, conscience, or moral responsibility to obey God rather than men (Acts 5:29). This submission warns against presumptive and inappropriate grasping after authority.[4]

Paul's third imperative further explains the meaning of submission. *A woman is to refrain from teaching or exercising authority over men in the assembly* (1 Tim. 2:12). Teaching in this context "has this restricted sense of authoritative doctrinal instruction."[5] Are women, then, barred from all teaching? Definitely not. Such a restriction would deprive others of being edified by women who have the gift of teaching. But the role of authoritative delivery of the Word to men is restricted *to men*. Douglas Moo adds that

> Paul's prohibition of women's having authority over a man would exclude a woman from becoming an elder in the way this office is described in the pastoral epistles. [We will learn about the responsibilities of elders in our next chapter.] . . .
>
> On the other hand, we do not think Paul's prohibition should restrict women from voting, with other men and women, in a congregational meeting, for, while the congregation as a whole can be said to be the final authority, this is not the same thing

4. Bruce B. Barton, David R. Veerman, and Neil Wilson, *1 Timothy, 2 Timothy, Titus*, Life Application Bible Commentary Series (Wheaton, Ill.: Tyndale House Publishers, 1993), p. 51.

5. Moo, "What Does It Mean Not to Teach or Have Authority Over Men?" p. 185.

as the exercise of authority ascribed, e.g., to the elders. Nor do we think Paul would intend to prohibit women from most church administrative activities.[6]

Why Is This Behavior Expected?

On what does Paul base these distinctions? Is he arbitrarily handing out assignments to men and women? Does he have a hidden agenda to keep women down, as some accuse? The next two verses provide the basis for Paul's instruction.

> For it was Adam who was first created, and then Eve. (v. 13)

Paul's model for the church is the order of Creation.

> The roles Paul spelled out here are a product of God's fundamental design wherein Adam was formed first, then Eve (cf. Gen. 2:7–25). More is involved here than mere chronological priority. Paul saw the priority in time as indicative of the leadership given to the male, to which the woman, the "helper suitable for him" (Gen. 2:18), should respond.[7]

Does this mean men are inherently better or more spiritual than women? Absolutely not, for both were created "in the image of God" (Gen. 1:27), and both are equal recipients of the grace of Christ (Gal. 3:28). "But in his sovereign wisdom," one commentator writes, "God made the human pair in such a manner that it is natural for *him* to lead, for *her* to follow."[8]

From Creation Paul next turns to the Fall.

> And it was not Adam who was deceived, but the woman being quite deceived, fell into transgression. (v. 14)

One commentary explains this verse as saying that

---

6. Moo, "What Does It Mean Not to Teach or Have Authority Over Men?" p. 187.

7. A. Duane Litfin, "1 Timothy," in *The Bible Knowledge Commentary*, New Testament edition, ed. John F. Walvoord and Roy B. Zuck (Wheaton, Ill.: Scripture Press Publications, Victor Books, 1983), pp. 735–36.

8. William Hendriksen, *Thessalonians, Timothy and Titus*, New Testament Commentary Series (Grand Rapids, Mich.: Baker Book House, 1979), p. 109.

Paul was not excusing Adam for his part in the Fall (Genesis 3:6–7, 17–19). On the contrary, in his letter to the Romans, Paul placed the primary blame for humanity's sinful nature on Adam (Romans 5:12–21). Eve had not been told directly by God about the trees—Adam had instructed her. In turn, God instructed Adam about the trees before Eve was created. For Eve, the struggle was over whether to submit to Adam's command or to the serpent's words that seemed to offer her knowledge and understanding. But when Adam ate of the fruit, he directly disobeyed God. He was not deceived; he sinned outright. By then, however, Eve had already sinned.

This verse should not be taken to prove that women are more gullible than men in general. In Ephesus, due to the persuasiveness of the male false teachers, some women *were* gullible. Paul didn't use this verse to say women were easily deceived, but to point out that Eve should have submitted to Adam in her particular situation.[9]

So far, Paul's instruction to women sounds like a string of negatives: "Don't teach; don't exercise authority." In what realm of responsibility does he see women shining the brightest?

But women shall be preserved through the bearing of children if they continue in faith and love and sanctity with self-restraint. (v. 15)

The Greek word translated *preserved* is the same term translated *saved* in other passages. Obviously, this can't mean eternal salvation in Christ. That only comes through faith, not by childbearing or any other human endeavor (see Eph. 2:8–10). What, then, does Paul mean?

Theologians have come up with many explanations, but the best interpretation seems to be that a woman is "saved" from wearing the label of "the one who was deceived" (1 Tim. 2:14) by performing the role God ordained for her in the first place. A. T. Robertson sums up this passage this way: "Child-bearing, not public teaching, is the peculiar function of woman with a glory and dignity

9. Barton, Veerman, and Wilson, *1 Timothy, 2 Timothy, Titus*, p. 54.

all its own."[10] Douglas Moo clarifies that

> the women with whom Paul is concerned in this paragraph are all almost certainly married, so that he can mention one central role—bearing and raising children—as a way of designating appropriate female roles generally.[11]

A Few Clarifying Remarks

Here are a few things to keep in mind as we conclude this study.

First a word to the men. *These role distinctions are to be gently respected, not exaggerated, expanded, or exploited.* Remember, Paul has been speaking in the context of the public worship service. So this passage doesn't give men license to dominate their wives or to imprison them behind the bars of silent subservience. Women are a cool spring of insight, wisdom, sensitivity, and creativity from which the opposite sex needs to drink deeply. If we forget that, we've taken role distinctions too far.

For the women, *your positive response to this instruction will help the church maintain its distinctives.* The church does not take its direction from the world. God wants Christian men and women to live in a way that reflects His character, His holiness, His Word—regardless of what the world says.

Finally, to everyone, *those who take their cues from the world will neither accept nor appreciate this teaching.* And listening to the world instead of the Word will lead to further confusion in the church.

 *Living Insights*

What an emotionally charged issue—for both sexes. One that makes it easy to let feelings, experiences, and background—instead of Scripture—determine the stand we take. What's your stand? The following few questions can help you clarify what you believe and why you believe it.

How would you describe your understanding and convictions

10. Archibald Thomas Robertson, *Word Pictures in the New Testament* (Grand Rapids, Mich.: Baker Book House, 1931), vol. 4, pp. 570–71.

11. Moo, "What Does It Mean Not to Teach or Have Authority Over Men?" p. 192.

on this issue at this point in your life?

_____

_____

_____

_____

_____

Has your perspective changed from previous beliefs? How and why?

_____

_____

_____

_____

What Scriptures have helped develop your understanding of this issue?

_____

_____

_____

How would you say your attitude about authority and submission in the Christian life measures up to Jesus' model in the following verses?

Matthew 11:27–30 _____

_____

Mark 10:42–45 _____

_____

Luke 6:31, 36–38 _____

_____

 ## Digging Deeper _____

As we've stated, an in-depth treatment of this topic lies beyond the scope of one chapter in a study guide. If you've been reading thoughtfully, you probably have some questions we didn't answer, such as:

- What about single women? Are they second-class citizens? Are they out of God's will because they're not raising a family?

- How can pastors, elders, and other church leaders promote role distinctions without coming across as chauvinists?

- How can women stand up for their dignity and resist oppression without coming across as feminists?

- Exactly what ministries, then, are legitimate for a woman to serve in or lead?

- If women aren't supposed to teach men, exactly when does a boy become a man? Can women teach or preach at youth camps, etc.?

For answering these and other important questions, we recommend, first of all, working through the passages listed earlier in this chapter. We also suggest that you pick up a couple of books that deal more thoroughly with the topic than we were able to do here. *Recovering Biblical Manhood and Womanhood: A Response to Evangelical Feminism,* edited by John Piper and Wayne Grudem (Wheaton, Ill.: Good News Publishers, Crossway Books, 1991); and *Women, Authority and the Bible,* edited by Alvera Mickelsen (Downers Grove, Ill.: InterVarsity Press, 1986) both contain excellent articles by leading evangelicals on key biblical passages.

Good studying. And remember, you'll learn a lot more from the Bible, and those who revere it, than you will from the bees.

Chapter 7

CHECKLIST FOR CHOOSING CHURCH LEADERS

1 Timothy 3:1–7

Death had crept over the Pride Lands like a gray-green shadow.

The ground, once covered with a mane of windswept grass and spotted with wild blossoms, now had the look of reptile skin left to dry and crack under the African sun. Brittle branches, the only remnants of vegetation, jutted from the parched land like lifeless claws. The earth once rumbled under the galloping hooves of antelope and wildebeest. But it was silent now, strewn with skulls and bones picked clean by hungry hyenas.

One lion was responsible for this desolation—Scar. He had usurped the throne by murdering his brother, King Mufasa, and driving Simba, the king's son and rightful heir, out of Pride Rock. And he had given free reign to the bitter enemies of Mufasa, the hyenas, allowing these trespassing scavengers to roam and ravage the countryside—their reward for helping Scar kill the king.

From a cliff on the outskirts of the Pride Lands, Simba, now a full-grown lion, scowled as he surveyed what was left of his homeland. The real king had at last returned. And it was time to take Pride Rock back. To do that, he must challenge Scar . . .

We won't spoil it for you. To find out how the story ends, you'll have to rent Walt Disney's record-breaking video *The Lion King*. Whether the film's creators intended it or not, *The Lion King* contains an important message about leadership: character matters at the top. Though Scar had the title of king, he didn't qualify for the position. He used the throne to feed his appetite for power and position rather than to care for his kingdom.

Abusive and irresponsible leadership exists in the real world too. A quick scan of history reveals a whole list of Scars—Jezebel, Herod, Nero, Hitler, Amin, Ceauşescu, Hussein—people with authority but no character. Instead of caring for their kingdoms, they led them into economic, cultural, and spiritual ruin.

Unfortunately, the secular world is not the only place with leadership problems. The body of Christ has its share too. Insecure and manipulative pastors and elders have ravaged congregations and split churches. Some leaders have trouble controlling their own passions; they can't lead themselves, much less others. Still others focus more on programs than personal holiness, creating a busy ministry that lacks the core of Christlikeness.

If you're a Christian leader, or if you have a part in choosing Christian leaders, you need to check out Paul's list of qualifications for selecting them in 1 Timothy 3:1–7. Following his checklist will help us choose the right men for leadership in our churches.

Erroneous Methods for Selecting Leaders

Before we study Paul's list, let's look at four ways *not* to select leadership.

Popularity

In far too many churches, charisma, visibility in the community, and professional success qualify an individual for leadership. The "up-front" types often appear the most confident, capable, and enthusiastic. Popularity alone, however, is an unreliable barometer for determining leadership skill, wisdom, or character.

The Past

Many congregations choose as leaders those who have been leaders in the past. "It's tradition to have a Jones on the elder board," Sam Jones might say. And as his father was an elder for forty years, so Sam wants to be for the next forty. "As it was in the beginning, is now and ever shall be, world without end. Amen, Amen" is his favorite hymn.[1] Churches that choose leaders by tradition rather than biblical qualifications end up with a board of great historians but poor visionaries. There's more to leading than "doing it the old way."

Politics

Some people get into leadership by slick political maneuvering. Pulling the right strings. Manipulating or massaging the right people. Shaking the right hands. Throwing around weight in the right places. It's not what you know (or who you are) that matters. It's who you know and how well you play the game. Congregations that allow such leaders to slip into office usually wake up to find

---

1. From the "Gloria Patri" ("Glory be to the Father"), in *The Hymnal for Worship and Celebration* (Waco, Tex.: Word Music, 1986), no. 623.

themselves exploited instead of edified.

Pocketbook

Money can't buy everything. But in some churches it can get you a seat on the elder board. No, we're not talking about bribery, but something more subtle. We often assume that, simply because a person has wealth, he qualifies for leadership. After all, someone with a track record of business success and generous giving must be doing something right.

Careful, though. Wealth doesn't necessarily signal integrity (nor a lack of it, for that matter). More important than financial success are character qualities such as humility and a teachable spirit— traits no amount of money could ever buy.

An Inerrant Checklist of Qualifications

Now let's take a look at God's criteria for leadership, beginning with two important facts about the context of 1 Timothy 3:1–7.

First, we must understand that this list applies to male candidates for the office of pastor or elder. Not that women don't or shouldn't demonstrate many of these same qualities. But Scripture limits this office to men. Men, after all, are to take the lead spiritually in the church (2:8, 12). Also, the references to being "the husband of one wife" (3:2a) and a manager of "his own household" (v. 4a) indicate that Paul has men in mind.

Second, these qualifications are essential, not optional. Note the imperative, "An overseer . . . must" (v. 2; see also vv. 4, 7). This passage presents a profile of a leader, not a pool of qualities from which to skim and pick. To qualify, an individual must meet all the criteria.

If we organize Paul's list into four main categories, we can appreciate the well-roundedness of the overseer, rather than viewing this passage as a random roster of individual terms. Paul addresses the overseer's personal or inner life (vv. 1–3), his home life (vv. 4–5), his church life (v. 6), and his life in the world of the unsaved (v. 7). We'll cover verses 1 and 2 in this lesson and the rest of the passage in the following chapter.

His Personal Life

Paul begins with a few words for those thinking about serving as leaders.

> It is a trustworthy statement: if any man aspires
> to the office of overseer, it is a fine work he desires
> to do. (v. 1)

It could be that the abuse of authority by some false teachers in Ephesus had tainted the image of church leadership. Or, as in our day, perhaps men were discouraged from pursuing a leadership position, having been told that the position should seek *them* out lest they appear overly ambitious. But Paul says, "You want to serve as an overseer? That's great! It's a fine office, an honorable position, and a noble intention."

What exactly is an "overseer"? Commentator Philip H. Towner helps us understand that term.

> The term translated *overseer* . . . was first used out-side the church to refer to supervisors of various sorts. As a description of one level of church leadership, it appears in Acts 20:28 and, again alongside "deacons," in Philippians 1:1. To judge from the account of Paul's farewell meeting with the elders (presbyters; compare 1 Tim. 5:17) of Ephesus (Acts 20:17–38) and the instructions in Titus 1:6–7, the terms "overseer" and "elder" referred to the same office. . . . Among the duties assigned to this office (though perhaps not exclusively) were preaching and teaching and generally leading or managing the church.[2]

Quite a responsibility for pastors and elders. So aspiration isn't enough. A man must qualify.

> An overseer, then, must be above reproach, the hus-band of one wife, temperate, prudent, respectable, hospitable, able to teach. (v. 2)

Let's look at each of these qualifications one by one.

1. First, an overseer must be *above reproach*, which doesn't mean he must be perfect, but that he

must have no flaw in his conduct that would be

2. Philip H. Towner, *1–2 Timothy and Titus* (Downers Grove, Ill.: InterVarsity Press, 1994), pp. 82–83.

grounds for any kind of accusation. He must be blameless. . . . A leader within the church should have a good reputation among believers.[3]

2. A good reputation includes being *the husband of one wife*. The text literally reads "one wife's husband." This requirement presents an interpretive challenge. Does it mean that an overseer must be a married man, or can he be single? If a man's wife dies and he remarries, is he disqualified? How does divorce affect his credentials? Is this a prohibition against polygamy? Duane Litfin explains:

> The question is, how stringent a standard was Paul erecting for overseers? Virtually all commentators agree that this phrase prohibits both polygamy and promiscuity, which are unthinkable for spiritual leaders in the church. Many Bible students say the words a "one-woman man" are saying that the affections of an elder must be centered exclusively on his wife. Many others hold, however, that the phrase further prohibits any who have been divorced and remarried from becoming overseers. The reasoning behind this view is usually that divorce represents a failure in the home, so that even though a man may be forgiven for any sin involved, he remains permanently disqualified for leadership in the congregation (cf. vv. 4–5; 1 Cor. 9:24–27).[4]

Each individual must of course develop his or her own position on this passage, but the spirit of Paul's words, as William Hendriksen says, is clear. An overseer

> must be a man of unquestioned morality, one who is entirely true and faithful to his one and only wife; one who, being married, does not in pagan fashion enter into an immoral relationship with another woman.[5]

3. Bruce B. Barton, David R. Veerman, and Neil Wilson, *1 Timothy, 2 Timothy, Titus*, Life Application Bible Commentary Series (Wheaton, Ill.: Tyndale House Publishers, 1993), p. 58.

4. A. Duane Litfin, "1 Timothy," *The Bible Knowledge Commentary*, New Testament edition, ed. John F. Walvoord and Roy B. Zuck (Wheaton, Ill.: Scripture Press Publications, Victor Books, 1983), p. 736.

5. William Hendriksen, *Thessalonians, Timothy, and Titus* (Grand Rapids, Mich.: Baker Book House, 1979), p. 121.

Before we appoint leaders, we need to make sure that, whether single or married, they exemplify moral purity and control.

3. An overseer should also be *temperate*. Paul has in mind here the "self-control necessary for effective ministry" (see also 3:11; Titus 2:2).[6] The Greek word, *nēphalios*, includes having a "clarity of mind," "soberness." Its root word, *nēphō*, means "the opposite of every kind of fuzziness. Sober judgment is highly valued in both individual and public life."[7]

In other words, an overseer avoids self-indulgence; and he's free from emotional extremism—balanced, not rash.

4. An overseer must also be *prudent* (1 Tim. 3:2). The Greek word is *sōphrōn*, literally, "of sound mind; self-controlled" which suggests wisdom and discretion.

Wisdom is more than the accumulation of biblical knowledge. It's the application of knowledge to the practicalities of life. It means exercising balanced judgment, avoiding both legalism and licentiousness. It also means having a grasp on the real world and drawing on the Word and personal experience to make decisions.

5. The next qualification, *respectable*, has several nuances:

> At first a philosophical term for the well-ordered and balanced person, this term later takes on a weaker social sense, "well-mannered" or "honorable."[8]

A man whose life displays the discipline and grace necessary for an overseer will gain the respect and honor of those whom he serves.

6. If you love to preach but can't stand people, you'll have trouble with this next requirement. An overseer must be *hospitable*. He must have an open heart and an open home. In the days of Timothy and Paul, hospitality was crucial to the survival of the church. From the first century until now many churches have met in homes for teaching and fellowship. Christians also took other believers into their homes to rescue them from persecution, provide shelter on a journey, or simply help them survive hardship.

---

6. *The New International Dictionary of New Testament Theology*, ed. Colin Brown (Grand Rapids, Mich.: Zondervan Publishing House, Regency Reference Library, 1986), vol. 1, p. 515.

7. Gerhard Kittel and Gerhard Friedrich, eds., *Theological Dictionary of the New Testament*, translated and abridged in one volume by Geoffrey W. Bromiley (reprint; 1985, Grand Rapids, Mich.: William B. Eerdmans Publishing Co., 1992), p. 634.

8. Kittel and Friedrich, eds., *Theological Dictionary of the New Testament*, trans. Bromiley, p. 464.

The church still needs hospitality. We're a family. We need to open our doors and hearts to share the joys, sorrows, and celebrations of others. Sometimes a struggling family needs shelter. Or a pregnant teenager needs a loving, supportive environment for herself and her baby. Others may just need encouragement.

What the church doesn't need are leaders who are aloof, unapproachable, and cold.

7. *Able to teach.* Does this mean that every leader should be an "up-front" type or someone who can launch into a forty-minute sermon on a moment's notice? Not at all. Duane Litfin explains that this phrase

> speaks of a leader's ability to handle the Scriptures. He must be able both to understand and to communicate the truth to others, as well as to refute those who mishandle it (cf. Titus 1:9). Not all must necessarily do this publicly, of course; some may conduct this aspect of their ministries more informally in private settings. Yet all leaders must possess an aptitude for handling the Word with skill.[9]

The Scriptures are central to ministry, as Paul says elsewhere in this same letter (1:3–11; 4:6, 11; 6:3–5). It's only natural, then, that ministry leaders should be skilled in handling the Word.

How unfortunate that the senior pastor is often the only one who can handle the Scriptures. All elders should be equipped to teach the Bible in a variety of contexts—in Sunday school, one-on-one discipleship and counseling, home study groups, and other venues.

Practical Suggestions for Application

Let's stop here and think about how to apply what we've learned so far. (We'll continue looking at Paul's list in the next lesson.)

First, *let's be careful in selecting leaders.* The worst thing we can do for a candidate, or for a church, is vote for him simply because we've known him a long time, or because we like his personality. Remember, it's character that counts. So try to get beyond the superficial. Make sure you know the person well enough to make a valid judgment.

Second, *let's be realistic.* While taking the selection of leaders

---

9. A. Duane Litfin, *The Bible Knowledge Commentary*, p. 737.

seriously, we must remember that no one's perfect. No one keeps the list 100 percent of the time. Every now and then, even the best leaders fail to love their wives as they should or occasionally let their emotions get the best of them. Paul's list, though binding and authoritative, must be seasoned with grace. Otherwise, none of us would be qualified to lead.

And third, *let's be aware and observant.* Keep your eyes open for prospective leaders. They aren't always extroverts. Sometimes they influence others through their consistent walk with God and their quiet servant spirit. Most leaders, in fact, don't rush to get their names on the ballot. They simply lead, then take the opportunities for ministry that come their way.

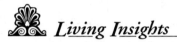 *Living Insights*

It's good that we have God's leadership list to go by. Otherwise, we would choose people with the most impressive credentials or the most pleasing personality. Though background and disposition are important, God's gaze probes far below the surface . . . to the heart.

> "For God sees not as man sees, for man looks at the outward appearance, but the Lord looks at the heart." (1 Sam. 16:7b)

God's not impressed with the ink on our resumes. He wants to know what's written on the heart. He's looking for the characteristics recorded in 1 Timothy 3:1–7.

Why do you suppose God has such high standards for leadership in His church?

_____

_____

What do these standards in 1 Timothy 3 tell you about:

• God's love for His church?_____

_____

• God's desire for His church's holiness? _____

_____

_____

- The importance of knowing people in your congregation?

_____

_____

- The accountability of leadership? _____

_____

_____

- The level of spiritual maturity in many churches today?

_____

_____

Chapter 8

ANOTHER LOOK
AT THE CHECKLIST

1 Timothy 3:1–7

So far, Paul's list in 1 Timothy 3 is quite impressive, isn't it? But instead of looking at it as an intimidating row of hurdles to jump over on the way to eldership, consider what it tells us about God and His character.

God knows what He wants; He's direct about righteousness, integrity, and faithfulness. You'll find no hazy generalities in this passage. And in this "anything goes" world, it should strengthen our hearts to know that we serve a God whose character and standards don't wobble in the winds of relativity and public opinion (see also Titus 1:5–9; 1 Pet. 5:1–4).

Notice, too, that Paul's list contains no reference to spiritual gifts, which means that God is more interested in leaders who evidence character than those who elevate spiritual gifts. As one Old Testament passage says,

> "For the eyes of the Lord move to and fro throughout
> the earth that He may strongly support those whose
> heart is completely His." (2 Chron. 16:9a)

God wants leaders whose hearts are set on Him, men who will do whatever it takes to represent righteousness.

> "And I searched for a man among them who should
> build up the wall and stand in the gap before Me
> for the land, that I should not destroy it; but I found
> no one." (Ezek. 22:30)

He's still searching for men to lead His church today—men who meet the requirements in 1 Timothy 3:1–7.

A Continuation of Leadership "Musts"

Last time, we looked at the seven qualifications listed in verse 2. Let's move on, then, to verses 3–7, where Paul lists the rest of the qualifications for overseer.

> . . . not addicted to wine or pugnacious, but gentle,
> uncontentious, free from the love of money. (v. 3)

Not Addicted to Wine

The Greek word for "addicted to wine" is *paroinos*. The parts
of the word, *para*, "beside," and *oinos*, "wine," describe a person who
spends too much time "beside the wine." In other words, under the
control of alcohol.

Overdrinking clouds the mind and blunts the senses—factors
that prohibit a leader from having a positive influence on the
church. For how can a man shepherd the flock if he becomes
mentally or emotionally unstable? And who can follow or respect
such an incapacitated leader?

Also, a problem with drinking suggests that a man has some
underlying needs he is avoiding rather than trying to face. He is
numbing himself to reality. How, then, can a man lead others into
truth when he's running from it himself (compare Ps. 51:6a)? If he
doesn't resolve his inner turmoil, his drinking will destroy his life
and slowly poison the church.

Drunkenness violates God's standard, not just for leaders but
for all Christians (read Rom. 13:12–14; 1 Cor. 5:11; Gal. 5:19–21;
Eph. 5:18; 1 Pet. 4:1–5). God wants us to be clear-thinking, alert,
and discerning individuals, capable of making sound decisions.

Not Pugnacious

The phrase *not pugnacious* literally means "not a striker."[1] Paul
is warning us away from someone who's quick with the blows,
physical or verbal, always looking for a good fight.

A pastor who uses the pulpit to scold individuals who disagree
with him or who consistently responds to criticism with defensive-
ness and anger has no business serving in leadership. Rather, a pastor
should model Jesus, who, instead of returning evil for evil, entrusted
judgment to His Father (see 1 Pet. 2:20–23).

Does this mean that a leader can't ever get angry or that he
should make pleasing people his priority? No. But a good leader
knows how to take heat without spreading the flames.

---

1. William Hendriksen, *Thessalonians, Timothy and Titus*, New Testament Commentary Series
(Grand Rapids, Mich.: Baker Book House, 1979), p. 125.

Gentle

The Greek word for *gentle*, *epieikes*, is also translated "yielding" or "forbearing." William Barclay underscores this trait's merciful side:

> Sometimes it may actually be unjust to apply the strict letter of the law. Trench said that *epieikeia* means "retreating from the letter of right better to preserve the spirit of right." . . . Aristotle describes in full the action of *epieikeia*: "To pardon human failings; to look to the law-giver, not to the law; to the intention, not to the action; to the whole, not to the part; to the character of the actor in the long run and not in the present moment; to remember good rather than evil, and the good that one has received rather than the good that one has done; to bear being injured; to wish to settle a matter by words rather than deeds." If there is a matter under dispute, it can be settled by consulting a book of practice and procedure, or it can be settled by consulting Jesus Christ. If there is a matter of debate, it can be settled in law, or it can be settled in love.[2]

A gentle leader doesn't demand his own way or lash out when he's treated unfairly. Nor does he feel threatened when others disagree with him. But neither does he let people walk all over him; if he did he wouldn't be a leader.

A gentle leader's words and actions are seasoned with grace, forgiveness, and kindness (reflect on John 8:1–11, which shows gentleness incarnated in Christ).

Uncontentious

The New International Version translates the Greek word as "not quarrelsome." Philip H. Towner explains that quarrelsomeness

> betrays an inability to get along with and accept the views of others, and perhaps deeper personality flaws as well. The false teachers in Ephesus were known for their quarrels (1:5; 6:4–5). A leader prone to this weakness will produce discord instead of

---

2. William Barclay, *The Letters to Timothy, Titus, and Philemon*, rev. ed., The Daily Study Bible Series (Philadelphia, Pa.: Westminster Press, 1975), pp. 83–84.

harmony. But a leader, or any Christian for that matter, who promotes peace among people will create and preserve the relationships necessary for building a unified church.[3]

Some leaders are, as Barclay puts it, "trigger-happy" in their relationships with others.[4] Quick on the draw, itching for a good argument. But a godly leader keeps his gun holstered until he needs it for the real enemy. He listens to others. He cooperates. He builds people up instead of tearing them down.

Free from the Love of Money

For too many people today, blessing and success are measured in dollars and cents. How misleading! Yet money itself isn't the problem. As author Gene Getz points out, it's our attitude toward it that gets us into trouble.

> The Scriptures do not teach that "money" per se is evil. Nor do they teach that it is wrong to have lots of money. What they do teach is that it is a serious violation of God's will when we *love it*. That is why Paul said that a mature Christian man is "free," not from money, but "from the love of money."[5]

Our attitude toward material wealth, Towner explains,

> ought to be one of healthy detachment, but certainly not irresponsibility. Such a leader can be a model of generosity and simplicity of lifestyle because of the knowledge that whatever one's economic status might be, all that one has belongs to God and so must be looked after faithfully before him (6:17–19).[6]

A godly leader loves God and uses money, not the other way around (see also Matt. 6:24; Titus 1:7; 1 Pet. 5:2).

3. Philip H. Towner, *1–2 Timothy and Titus*, The IVP New Testament Commentary Series (Downers Grove, Ill.: InterVarsity Press, 1994), p. 87.

4. Barclay, *The Letters to Timothy, Titus, and Philemon*, p. 84.

5. Gene A. Getz, *The Measure of a Man* (Ventura, Calif.: Gospel Light Publications, Regal Books, 1995), p. 193.

6. Towner, *1–2 Timothy and Titus*, p. 87.

One Who Manages His Own Household Well

It is significant that Paul's only reference to management in this passage concerns the home, not the business world. Leading the church certainly involves management—of time, priorities, staff, programs, and more, but Paul's focus is on the home and family.

> He must be one who manages his own household well, keeping his children under control with all dignity (but if a man does not know how to manage his own household, how will he take care of the church of God?). (1 Tim. 3:4–5)

Why? Because the church is a family, not a business. It has a heavenly Father, not a chairman of the board. Brothers and sisters, not shareholders. We have a Groom, Jesus Christ, not an impersonal boss.

Here's the straight scoop: It doesn't matter if a man succeeds at everything else in life. If he's not leading his family well, he's disqualified from leading the church. Far too many men are up to their kneecaps in business, church work, and other endeavors—and often enjoying success in all these areas. But their homes are in disarray. If you want to know how a man is going to lead the church, look at his home life.

A word of caution, though: nobody's home is going to be perfect twenty-four hours a day. Even the preacher's kid is going to run down the aisle of the grocery store now and then. So what we need to look for is the general tenor of the home. Are the kids respectful, the home well-ordered? Are the parents attentive, involved, and supportive of each other and their children? How is the communication? Is an atmosphere of spiritual development being fostered? Is Jesus Christ openly discussed and revered? Is the Word studied?

A man who has these priorities for his family will make a leader worth following.

Not a New Convert

> And not a new convert, lest he become conceited and fall into the condemnation incurred by the devil. (v. 6)

An overseer must not be a "neophyte," literally, which means "newly planted."[7] The role of an elder calls for roots. It calls for

---

7. Hendriksen, *Thessalonians, Timothy and Titus*, p. 127.

perception, experience, wisdom. It calls for someone who has been seasoned by life's triumphs, failures, joys, and disappointments.

A brand-new believer, right out of the spiritual womb, can easily fall victim to discouragement or, on the other hand, pride. Only the growing pains of maturity produce stability and a humble heart.

A Good Reputation with Those outside the Church

> And he must have a good reputation with those outside the church, so that he may not fall into reproach and the snare of the devil. (v. 7)

Are you surprised to find this qualification on the list? After all, what does the surrounding community have to do with choosing leaders in the church? Well, the world observes the candidate's lifestyle too. And remember, reputation matters.

Is this man friendly? How does he handle conflict, disagreement? How did he respond when the neighbor's kid knocked a ball through the living room window? How does he treat the dry cleaner, the grocery checker, and the waitress? We can often discover a lot about a man from neighbors who have nothing to gain or lose from his appointment to leadership.

It's important, though, to understand that some people dislike Christians simply because they're Christians. So feedback from neighbors, as all input, must be received with discretion.

A Few Questions regarding Potential Leaders

Well, that's Paul's profile for elders. In the next chapter, we'll take a look at what it takes to serve as a deacon in the church. Let's wrap up with three questions we should ask of those who want to serve in any facet of leadership.

Personally, do his internals square with his externals? He speaks well in public. He's well-mannered and neat. He handles himself well under pressure. But does his inner character measure up to his outward appearance?

Domestically, would his family vote for him? How would a candidate's wife and kids respond? Would they agree that he "manages his own household well"? Or does the home function in spite of him?

Publicly, will the community be surprised or affirming? Would people in his work place nod and smile at the news of his nomination? Or would they look puzzled and ask, "Wait a minute. Are we talking about the same guy?"

Extensive qualifications? Yes. Unreasonable? No. They tell us that God takes leadership seriously. The Good Shepherd loves His sheep too much to leave us unprotected. And character is the best defense against wolves.

 ## Living Insights

Paul's list provides an important principle for these days when so many church leaders are spiraling down to ruin like smoking planes: All leading begins with following. Following God, that is. Each of the qualities on Paul's list—moral purity, hospitality, gentleness, sobriety, and so on—sprout from a nourishing, obedient relationship with Jesus Christ. As we follow Him, His Spirit produces these qualities in our lives.

As Jonathan Edwards wrote:

> [Ministers] should earnestly seek after much of the spiritual knowledge of Christ, and that they may live in the clear views of his glory. For by this means they will be changed into the image of the same glory and brightness, and will come to their people, as Moses came down to the congregation of Israel . . . with his face shining. If the light of Christ's glory shines upon them, it will be the way for them to shine with the same kind of light on their hearers, and to reflect the same beams, which have heat, as well as brightness. . . . Ministers should be much in seeking God, and conversing with him by prayer, who is the fountain of light and love.[8]

Henri Nouwen puts this truth in a different and direct way:

> A Christian minister will never be able to be a minister if it is not his own most personal faith and insight into life that forms the core of his pastoral work.
> So, ministry and spirituality never can be separated. Ministry is not an eight-to-five job but primarily a way of life.[9]

8. Iain H. Murray, *Jonathan Edwards: A New Biography* (1987; reprint, Carlisle, Pa.: Banner of Truth Trust, 1992), p. 144.

9. Henri J. M. Nouwen, *Creative Ministry* (Garden City, N.Y.: Doubleday and Co., 1971), p. xx.

Are you a leader? Are you spending adequate time with Christ? Enriching your soul so you can enrich others? If you need to, what adjustments can you make in your schedule to allow for this?

_____

_____

_____

_____

What about other leaders in your church? How can you encourage them or help free them up to spend more time in the presence of the Lord?

_____

_____

_____

_____

The power for ministry doesn't rest in programs; it rests in a Person. So let's lead, first of all, by following Him.

> Then he answered and said to me, "This is the word of the Lord to Zerubbabel saying, 'Not by might nor by power, but by My Spirit,' says the Lord of hosts." (Zech. 4:6)

Chapter 9

THE DIGNITY OF SERVANTHOOD

1 Timothy 3:8–13

Nominations are now open for deacons. Here are the qualifications:

Must be able to pass the offering plate with a smile and without spilling.

Evidences the spiritual gift of *donukopheia*—a relentless passion to serve doughnuts and coffee after the worship service.

Looks good in a name tag.

Driven by a desire to do the stuff no one else wants to do.

Sounds trite, doesn't it? It is. Such caricatures of the deacon's role veil the true dignity and significance of the position. We often prop our pastors and elders up on pedestals. But deacons? Well, they're somewhere down below . . . dusting the pedestal. Deacons, we assume, are merely those who can't preach, teach, or lead. So they're relegated to the life of a holy "go-fer," performing the tasks others view as insignificant or non-spiritual.

How untrue to Scripture. Though deacons do perform many of the "nuts and bolts" ministries of the church, God sees their role—and all forms of service—as worthy of respect and honor. You might even be surprised to find that the qualifications for deacon and elder are essentially the same, which confirms that God wants all those who serve in His church to exhibit the character of Christ Himself.

Deacon: A God-Given Title

We find deacons recorded as early as Acts 6, where the church realized that a handful of leaders couldn't meet all the needs of a growing congregation.

Now at this time while the disciples were

increasing in number, a complaint arose on the part of the Hellenistic Jews against the native Hebrews, because their widows were being overlooked in the daily serving of food. And the twelve summoned the congregation of the disciples and said, "It is not desirable for us to neglect the word of God in order to serve tables. But select from among you, brethren, seven men of good reputation, full of the Spirit and of wisdom, whom we may put in charge of this task. But we will devote ourselves to prayer, and to the ministry of the word." And the statement found approval with the whole congregation; and they chose Stephen, a man full of faith and of the Holy Spirit, and Philip, Prochorus, Nicanor, Timon, Parmenas and Nicolas, a proselyte from Antioch. And these they brought before the apostles; and after praying, they laid their hands on them. (Acts 6:1–6)

The Hellenistic widows were hungry. And the ministry of food distribution called for someone caring and attentive to their needs. But the apostles, who were acting as overseers, needed to stay focused on their primary ministry of prayer and teaching the Word.

So the apostles had the congregation select seven men to serve tables (v. 2–3). The word *serve* in the Greek is *diakoneo*, from which we get our word *deacon*.[1] A deacon, then, in the context of this passage, is one who serves in a way that meets the physical needs of the congregation. But the role of these seven men should dispel any notion that servanthood is a menial job.

Notice, first of all, the qualifications presented by the apostles — a good reputation, full of the Holy Spirit, and wise. Can't anyone pass out food? The apostles didn't think so. They wanted responsible, godly, honest men to carry out this ministry.

Consider also the results of their ministry. The widows were fed. The body experienced the joy of serving one another. The teaching ministry of the apostles continued without interruption. And the church retained its reputation as a caring community. All because seven men served faithfully.

By the time Paul wrote to the Philippians, the role of deacon

---

1. Robert L. Thomas, ed., *New American Standard Exhaustive Concordance of the Bible* (Nashville, Tenn.: Holman Bible Publishers, 1981), p. 1642.

had become an office in the local church (see Phil. 1:1). So now local assemblies were recognizing the need for an official ministry that met the physical needs of the congregation and allowed the elders to focus on spiritual leadership.

Deacons aren't second-class citizens; they are themselves ministers of God. And, like elders, they are to be chosen according to the criteria laid out in God's Word.

Deacon: An Analysis of True Servants

Let's turn, then, to 1 Timothy 3:8 and discover the qualifications to consider in choosing deacons.

> Deacons likewise must be men of dignity, not double-tongued, or addicted to much wine or fond of sordid gain, but holding to the mystery of the faith with a clear conscience. And let these also first be tested; then let them serve as deacons if they are beyond reproach. (3:8–10)

Men of Dignity

The word "likewise" (v. 8) tells us that Paul is prescribing the same high standards for deacons as he did for elders in verses 1–7. Deacons, too, must be chosen carefully, according to their character—not randomly recruited.

A "man of dignity" is a man of serious and worthy conduct.[2] In other words, not frivolous, shallow, superficial, or silly. This doesn't mean deacons aren't allowed to have fun or possess a sense of humor. But they should take to their role with determination, commitment, and stability.

Not Double-Tongued

Commentator William Barclay explains that the Greek word

> *dilogos* means *speaking with two voices*, saying one thing to one and another to another. . . . A deacon, in his going from house to house, and in his dealing with those who needed charity, had to be a

2. Gerhard Kittel and Gerhard Friedrich, eds., *Theological Dictionary of the New Testament*, one-volume edition, trans. Geoffrey W. Bromiley, (Grand Rapids, Mich.: William B. Eerdmans Publishing Co.; Devon, UK: Pater Noster Press, 1985), p. 1014.

straight man. Again and again he would be tempted to evade issues by a little timely hypocrisy and smooth speaking. But the man who would do the work of the Christian Church must be straight.[3]

This characteristic also suggests that deacons keep a confidence. In the scope of their service, they will be trusted with information from other church members, much of which is sensitive and secret. Deacons should be trustworthy and discerning enough to know what to keep and what to share.

Not Addicted to Much Wine

Drunkenness is prohibited for deacons, just as it is for elders (3:3). A deacon under the influence of alcohol can't adequately serve the body or model Christlike devotion before the rest of the congregation.

Not Fond of Sordid Gain

The *New International Version* renders this phrase "not pursuing dishonest gain." The love of money disqualifies deacons as well as elders. But the emphasis here, as William Hendriksen explains, is slightly different from that of 3:3.

> A man who is fond of money is not necessarily an embezzler. But it is the embezzler or pilferer and the man who joins a good cause for the sake of material advantage whom Paul has in mind here in v. 8. It is the man with the mercenary spirit who goes all out in his search for riches, anxious to add to his possessions regardless of the method, whether fair or foul.[4]

Considering that, in many churches, the collection and sorting of the offering is handled by deacons, this is no small criteria.

Holding to the Mystery of the Faith with a Clear Conscience

Deacons must have spiritual depth. Specifically, says Duane Litfin,

---

3. William Barclay, *The Letters to Timothy, Titus and Philemon* (Philadelphia, Pa.: Westminster Press, 1975), pp. 85-86.

4. William Hendriksen, *Thessalonians, Timothy and Titus* (Grand Rapids, Mich.: Baker Book House, 1957), p. 131.

they should be men who understand and hold fast the deep truths of the faith. By the phrase **with a clear conscience** Paul (cf. "good conscience" in 1 Tim. 1:5) meant that there must be nothing in the conduct of these men that was glaringly inconsistent with their professed beliefs. In other words they must not profess one thing but practice another.[5]

Did you catch that? God's Word changes lives. In fact, those who are exposed to it and remain unchanged fall short of the qualifications for deacon. You see, God doesn't just want to plug warm bodies into church programs. He wants living, breathing models of His revealed truth.

Tested, Then Approved

God considers serving as a deacon so important, He wants candidates to be tested first. The Greek word for *test, dokimazo,* means "to test in the hope of being successful."[6] Paul isn't describing a squint-eyed scrutiny fueled by suspicion, but observation with the anticipation of approval. One commentary further explains that *testing*

> refers not to some formal testing but rather to observation by those who appoint deacons. The candidate will have shown the required moral characteristics and approved doctrine (3:9) consistently in the ordinary activities of church membership. A man who has proven his quality over time can then serve as a deacon. Testing deacons is needed today. They should not be appointed without consideration of their doctrine and their Christian life.[7]

Deacons have to do more than fill a slot and pass the plate. First they have to pass the test.

5. A. Duane Litfin, "1 Timothy" in *The Bible Knowledge Commentary,* ed. John F. Walvoord and Roy B. Zuck (Wheaton, Ill.: Victor Books, 1983), p. 738.

6. Donald Guthrie, *The Pastoral Epistles* (Grand Rapids, Mich.: William B. Eerdmans Publishing Co., 1990), p. 96.

7. Bruce B. Barton, David R. Veerman, Neil Wilson, *1 Timothy, 2 Timothy, Titus,* Life Application Bible Commentary Series (Wheaton, Ill.: Tyndale House Publishers, 1993) p. 68.

Women . . . Likewise

Women must likewise be dignified, not malicious gossips, but temperate, faithful in all things. (v. 11)

The Greek word for *woman* here is *gyne*, which is translated both "woman" and "wife" in the New Testament.[8] To whom, then, does verse 11 apply? Is Paul referring to 1) the wives of deacons, 2) all women in the church, or 3) female deacons, deaconesses?

The third option seems the most likely, for several reasons. First, notice the term "likewise." Paul uses this term to link items in a series (see v. 8). In this context, Paul is dealing with positions in the church. It seems natural that he would include deaconesses along with elders and deacons, rather than dealing with women in general.

Second, the pronoun "their" is conspicuously absent in the Greek text. It seems that Paul would have spoken of "their wives" if he were referring to the spouses of deacons.

Finally, Scripture contains several examples of women who served faithfully in the early church. Consider, for example, Phoebe (Rom. 16:1), Priscilla (Rom. 16:3), and Lydia (Acts 16:14–15). Such a record of vital contributions seems to allow for the office of deaconess.

Deaconesses, then, are held to the same standard of character as deacons. Their conversation and lifestyle must reflect the qualities of a mature believer.

Husband of One Wife

Deacons, just like elders, are called to a high standard of marital fidelity and moral purity.

Good Managers of the Home

As with elders, the measuring stick for good management is the home, not the business. A deacon who exercises his authority with love, wisdom, orderliness, and a servant's heart will bring those same qualities to the church.

---

8. Kittel, p. 134.

Deacon: Respect and Reward

Deacons and deaconesses serve faithfully over time; they serve diligently and well; they're significant in the life of the church. So what can they expect in return for their service? Thunderous applause? Rarely. High visibility? Occasionally, perhaps. Promotion to elder? No doubt many successful deacons will make successful elders. But deacons shouldn't look for such temporal rewards. Their greatest rewards are spiritual.

> For those who have served well as deacons obtain for themselves a high standing and great confidence in the faith that is in Christ Jesus. (v. 13)

Duane Litfin explains this verse as follows:

> Though the position of deacon seems by worldly standards to be menial and unattractive, to close followers of Jesus Christ it looks quite different (cf. John 13:11–17; Mark 10:42–45). Those who fulfill their servant roles faithfully gain two things: first, an excellent standing before fellow Christians who understand and appreciate the beauty of humble, selfless, Christlike service; and second, great assurance . . . in their faith in Christ Jesus. Humble service, which lacks all the rewards the world deems important, becomes a true test of one's motives.[9]

Deacons and deaconesses serve in silence much of the time. But remember what the greatest Servant of all time said?

> "For who is greater, the one who reclines at the table, or the one who serves? Is it not the one who reclines at the table? But I am among you as the one who serves." (Luke 22:27)

He also said

> "But many who are first will be last; and the last, first." (Matt. 19:30)

Servanthood. It has a dignified ring to it, don't you think?

---

9. Litfin, p. 738.

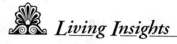 *Living Insights*

You don't have to hold the office of deacon in order to serve. Some people serve the body as teachers, pastors, elders, or staff members. Others serve by singing in the choir, greeting visitors, or maintaining the church grounds. All of us, though, should be serving in the body to some degree. That's why the church is called "the body of Christ." We're all interconnected; each one of us has something to offer that will benefit the whole.

Are you currently serving somehow in your local church?

_____

_____

_____

If not, in what ways would you most like to minister?

_____

_____

_____

What can you do this week to begin serving the body?

_____

_____

_____

It's your serve.

Chapter 10

A HOPE, A HOUSE, A HYMN

1 Timothy 3:14–16

Rules are best understood in the context of experience.

A curious toddler, for example, hears the repeated warning, "Stay away from that barbecue grill—hot!" To the child, this sounds like a cruel restriction, an obstacle to world exploration . . . until he touches the grill. Suddenly, and painfully, the rule makes sense to the little guy. "Hot" is seared into his memory and vocabulary forever. And he discovers that Mommy and Daddy's rules actually have some connection to real life.

Right now you may feel like that toddler, bound by a string of clinical commands threaded through 1 Timothy. "Men should . . . Women should . . . An overseer must . . . Deacons must . . . Deaconesses must." But don't despair. Paul's about to reveal the reasons behind the roster. And they actually relate to real life in the church.

Paul's Hope: A Reunion with Timothy

Lest we forget that Paul's instructions flow from a deep friendship with Timothy, the apostle expresses his hope of seeing his friend again.

> I am writing these things to you, hoping to come to you before long. (v. 14)

In the midst of teaching about "these things"—false doctrines, the power of the gospel, prayer, men's and women's roles, qualifications for leadership, and so on—Paul lets his personal side shine through. We often recognize Timothy's need for Paul—the young pastor sitting at the feet of the embattled apostle, the disciple under the tutelage of the discipler. But verse 14 reveals something about Paul's need for Timothy. A smile must have stretched across Paul's face as he scratched these words on parchment, thinking about seeing his dear son in the faith and hearing how God had been working in Ephesus.

God's House: The Church of Jesus Christ

Our plans don't always turn out the way we design them. Knowing this, Paul communicated with Timothy by letter, in the event a face-to-face talk might be delayed. What was so important that it couldn't wait until a visit? Look at verse 15.

> I write so that you may know how one ought to conduct himself in the household of God, which is the church of the living God, the pillar and support of the truth.

The communication of proper conduct in the church—that's the purpose of Paul's letter in a nutshell. Don't glide over that statement too quickly. How a church behaves, as William Barclay points out, reveals the reality of its faith.

> The word for *behave* is *anastrephesthai*; it describes what we might call a man's walk and *conversation*. It describes his whole life and character; but it specially describes him in his relationships with other people. As it has been said the word in itself lays it down that a church member's personal character must be excellent and that his personal relationships with other people should be a true fellowship. A church congregation is a body of people who are friends with God and friends with each other.[1]

To Paul, "behaving in church" doesn't mean keeping the kids from fidgeting during the sermon. It means that Christians, who have become part of God's household, should live by His house rules.

When Paul calls the church the *household of God*, he isn't referring to a building; he's talking about the relationship of the members of the household to one another and to the Master of the house. Philip H. Towner explains:

> The Greco-Roman household consisted of different groups, duties and responsibilities, and in the larger ones stewards were given authority to see that each

---

1. William Barclay, *The Letters to Timothy, Titus, and Philemon* (Philadelphia, Pa.: Westminster Press, 1975), p. 88.

did her or his share so that the master's purposes might be achieved. The concept of household with its associated notions of interdependence, acceptable conduct and responsibility was so strong that Paul could borrow it to illustrate the nature of the church. It too, both then and now, is made of different groups (men and women from every level of society, parents and children, employers and employees) who must depend upon and, in love, serve one another, and it is the task of the stewards (bishops/elders, deacons) to ensure that the household accomplishes the Master's goals.[2]

In other words, the church is a family. Not a corporation, not a program, but a tightly knit family. Brothers and sisters, sons and daughters of the same Father.

Paul's use of the phrase *church of the living God* reminds us of the church's uniqueness. The church is an assembly, called out from the world to be distinct in holiness and purpose.

Finally, the church is the *pillar and support of the truth*. The word *pillar* would have had special significance to the Ephesians, in whose city stood the extravagant temple of the goddess Diana.

[The temple] was one of the seven wonders of the world. One of its features was its pillars. It contained one hundred and twenty-seven pillars, every one of them the gift of a king. All were made of marble, and some were studded with jewels and overlaid with gold. The people of Ephesus knew well how beautiful a thing a pillar could be.[3]

Yet the pillars were more than mere objects of beauty.

It may well be that the idea of the word *pillar* here is not so much *support* . . . as *display*. . . . The idea here is that the Church's duty is to hold up the truth in such a way that all men may see it.

The buttress is the support of the building. It keeps it standing intact. In a world which does not

2. Philip H. Towner, *1–2 Timothy and Titus* (Downers Grove, Ill.; InterVarsity Press, 1994), p. 94.

3. Barclay, p. 89.

wish to face the truth, the Church holds it up for all to see. In a world which would often gladly eliminate unwelcome truth, the Church supports it against all who would seek to destroy it.[4]

Paul's Hymn: A Statement of Faith

Paul's discussion of truth and the family of God leads him into a hymn that centers on the person and ministry of Christ, who is the reason for all instructions on church behavior.

> And by common confession great is the mystery of godliness:
>
> > He who was revealed in the flesh,
> > Was vindicated in the Spirit,
> > Beheld by angels,
> > Proclaimed among the nations,
> > Believed on in the world,
> > Taken up in glory.
> > (v. 16)

The phrase introducing the hymn, "by common confession," suggests that what follows was familiar to Paul's readers.

What his readers "commonly confess" is the greatness of *the mystery of godliness*. Paul often used the word *mystery* in reference to Christ's appearance in history as God's hidden plan of salvation.

"This phrase *the mystery of godliness*," we're told by Towner, "forms a connection between the appearance of Christ . . . and Christian living: *the mystery* is the essence of *godliness*."[5] In other words, Christ Himself is the secret to proper Christian behavior. Success in the Christian life stems from a person, not programs or formulas.

And what a Person He is, as the hymn reveals. Jesus Christ came to earth as the God-man, deity clothed in human flesh. He proclaimed the message of God's grace and forgiveness, a message we continue to spread today that people might be saved. After His death and resurrection, Christ ascended to heaven amid the celebration of angels, who, years earlier, had announced His birth. And

4. Barclay, p. 89.

5. Towner, p. 98.

the sending of His Spirit confirmed that He had risen and taken His place at the right hand of the Father.

A great and glorious mystery indeed!

Three Final Thoughts

Let's wrap up with three final thoughts that can help us apply this passage into our daily lives.

First, *we should base our conduct on scriptural principles, not our own desires.* Paul didn't leave Timothy to pastor on mere intuition or emotion. He wrote so Timothy would know how to live and lead in the household of God (3:15). And God has preserved that letter so that we, too, have principles to live by.

Second, *the church is to confirm and model the truth, not invent its own message.* Methods, of course, change from age to age and culture to culture. But God's Word never changes. If we alter the gospel, or contrive our own plan for the church, then *we* become the standard instead of God's infallible Word.

Third, *our confession of faith revolves around Jesus Christ and no one else.* He is the center and source of our belief. Our doctrine, our bylaws, and our programs should all be based on Christ and His message, not tradition or assumption.

First Timothy may look like a rule book for the church. But remember, these are no ordinary rules. They're rooted in the Redeemer.

 Living Insights

Some people see the Christian life as a new set of rules to follow. That's partially true. As believers, our standard is the Bible. But someone can agree with and even endeavor to follow biblical principles and still not be a Christian. The Christian life begins with, and depends on, a Person. Jesus Himself put it this way:

> "I am the vine, you are the branches; he who abides
> in Me, and I in him, he bears much fruit; for apart
> from Me you can do nothing." (John 15:5)

Once we're grounded in a relationship with the living Lord, His commands are no longer burdensome (Matt. 11:28–30). Our days of slavish rule-keeping are over. Once we belong to Him, we're meant to delight in pleasing Him.

Take some time to evaluate your own spiritual walk. Are you scrambling to keep rules or do you desire to obey the Lord out of a deep love for Him and passion to please Him?

If you answered the former, maybe you need a reminder that the Christian life is a relationship, not a performance. Read the following passages, and write down what they tell you about your relationship with Christ.

John 15:4–5 _____

_____

_____

_____

Psalm 23 _____

_____

_____

_____

John 10:7–18 _____

_____

_____

Romans 8:31–39 _____

_____

_____

_____

The next time you start to see the Christian life as an impossible "to do" list, come back to these verses . . . for a personal visit.

Chapter 11

MINISTERING AMIDST
THE *CRAZIES*
1 Timothy 4:1–6

The yellow page ad, bordered in bold red, proved that there's a niche for everyone.

Metaphysical Fellowship Church
Services Friday 8 P.M., Sunday 7 P.M.
Psychic development classes Mon.–Thurs. 7:30 P.M.
First Saturday of the month is psychic day.

These are crazy times. Anything goes, it seems. The more outrageous, the more popular. The wackier, the better. That applies to music, movies, fashion . . . and religion.

Should one feel the compulsion to consult a long dead king, celebrity, or relative, there's a church just for that person. Those who would rather chant, shave their heads, and rattle a tambourine can easily find a group where they'll feel right at home. Even among conservative churches you can find all kinds of behaviors taken to an extreme. Worship services include wild laughter, and even barking.

Aberrant doctrines and practices abound. To those committed to Christ, this is, and should be appalling. But take comfort that God is neither surprised nor unnerved by the existence of "the crazies." In fact, He predicted their appearance, and they cropped up right on schedule.

Paul's letter to Timothy broaches the topic of these misled people and offers us clues for recognizing them and advice for avoiding their mistakes. Let's take a look at 1 Timothy 4:1–6.

The Certainty of Apostasy

Departure from God's truth has a name: apostasy. Paul warns Timothy that apostasy is not only possible, it is inevitable.

> But the Spirit explicitly says that in later times some
> will fall away from the faith. (1 Tim. 4:1a)

That literary link "but" connects us with the hymn in 3:16, the "common confession" of Christ's followers. That hymn is a list of the basic truths and tenets of Christianity, remember? And now Paul is presenting a contrast between those who hold to the truths of Christ and those who fall away from them. The Greek word for "fall away," *aphistemi*, carries the idea of abandoning the truth and "capitulat[ing] to heretical beliefs."[1]

So in chapter 3, Paul reminded Timothy—and us—that the purpose of the church is to uphold the truths of Christ. Now he warns us about those who let go of those truths—and worse, those who will deny and distort them. The "later times," or church age, has been and will always be characterized, not only by the light of God's Word, but by the accompanying shadow of apostasy (see also Mark 13:21–22; Acts 20:28–31; 2 Thess. 2:1–3; 2 Pet. 3:3, 17; Jude 18–19).

The Components of Apostasy

But what exactly constitutes apostasy? Is it always as obvious as the glazed stares of the crystal-gazers or the sheared heads and flowing robes of street-corner Hari Krishnas? Or can it be more subtle? What are apostasy's earmarks, and where does it begin? Let's find out.

Sourced in Satan

To begin with, apostasy bears the marks of Satan himself, who has been distorting God's truth since the garden of Eden (see Gen. 3:1–5). As Paul boldly tells us, those who reject Christ are "paying attention to deceitful spirits and doctrines of demons" (v. 1b).

Be careful, though. Not every false doctrine comes packaged with a label that reads DANGER: SATANIC DOCTRINE EN-CLOSED. OPEN AT YOUR OWN RISK. False teaching is often promulgated by attractive, friendly, convincing individuals. That's why we need to know the Scriptures—so we can discern truth from error, no matter how clever falsehood's disguise.

Encouraged by False Teachers

God and Satan have one thing in common—they both employ people to carry out their purposes. God delivers truth through people, but Satan delivers falsehood. And he does it

---

1. Gerhard Kittel and Gerhard Friedrich, *Theological Dictionary of the New Testament*, one volume edition (Grand Rapids, Mich.: William B. Eerdmans Publishing Company; Exeter, Devon, UK: Paternoster Press Ltd., 1985), trans. Geoffrey W. Bromiley, p. 88.

by means of the hypocrisy of liars seared in their own conscience as with a branding iron. (v. 2)

As Duane Litfin explains, God's enemies work through

hypocritical liars (lit., "men who speak lies in hypocrisy"). This is Satan's standard operating procedure (cf. 2 Cor. 11:13–15). He selects likely representatives and renders their consciences beyond feeling (cf. Eph. 4:19), seared (from *kausteriazo*, "to brand, cauterize") as with a hot iron. In this condition they are ready to do Satan's bidding.[2]

Do you ever wonder why so many cults are successful in seducing people to join them? It's because their spokespersons are "seared" in their conscience. They're convinced that they're teaching truth, and their confident assertions sway those who lack a solid biblical foundation.

Don't ever buy the misleading line that "doctrine isn't important for the Christian; it's a personal relationship with Christ that counts." Knowing God is directly related to knowing what He has revealed. Devotion is based on doctrine. And that's what cults and other false teachers attack. Sadly, too many Christians have a flimsy understanding of such vital doctrines as Christ's atonement, His deity, the Trinity, the sinfulness of man, and the holiness of God. A firm grip on these and other biblical truths is crucial if we're to drown out the seductive whispers of apostasy.

Characterized by Extremes

Non-scriptural extremism often characterizes false teaching. Such imbalance proceeds from

men who forbid marriage and advocate abstaining from foods, which God has created to be gratefully shared in by those who believe and know the truth. For everything created by God is good, and nothing is to be rejected, if it is received with gratitude; for it is sanctified by means of the word of God and prayer. (vv. 3–5)

2. A. Duane Litfin, "First Timothy" in *The Bible Knowledge Commentary* (Wheaton, Ill.: Victor Books, 1983), ed. John F. Walvoord and Roy B. Zuck, p. 739.

The errant teaching weaving its way through Ephesus was most likely an early form of Gnosticism. Commentators Barton, Veerman, and Wilson explain that these

> false teachers, perhaps under Jewish influence, gave stringent rules forbidding marriage and demanding abstinence from certain foods. Later, these teachings became part of what we know as Gnosticism—a belief that spirit is good, but the physical world is evil. Thus anything done for the body's pleasure or to fulfill its needs (such as sex or eating) was evil. To be "good" and to achieve a higher spiritual state, a person must deny all evil, including natural physical desires.[3]

How contrary to the nature of God, who called all of His creation "good" (see Gen. 1:4, 10, 12, 18, 21, 25, 31). Any religious system based on something other than God's truth will try to make up for the deficiency with counterfeit piety, such as the avoidance of practices that God has provided for our enjoyment and nurture.

Those who "know and believe the truth" should graciously enjoy everything that God has given. How could God hate sex, for instance, when He's the one who invented it? Husbands and wives are to enjoy that aspect of their relationship. And, though we should avoid gluttony, God has given us all kinds of food to enjoy. Why else would he make such varied sources of delectable taste and necessary nutrition available to us?

Sure, we need to be discerning about what enters our eyes, ears, mouths, hearts, and minds. But that doesn't mean we can't appreciate fine art, relish good music, savor tasty cooking, or read excellent literature. The only stipulation is that we receive God's gifts thankfully and with the awareness that He is at the center of everything we do (see also Col. 3:16–23).

Confronting Apostasy

Apostasy will always be with us, this side of heaven anyway. People within our own camp will buy into false doctrine and abandon the faith. So how do we fight apostasy? How do we resist it?

---

3. Bruce B. Barton, David R. Veerman, and Neil Wilson, *Life Application Bible Commentary: 1 Timothy, 2 Timothy and Titus* (Wheaton, Ill.: Tyndale House Publishers, 1993), p. 77.

Tell It like It Is

> In pointing out these things to the brethren, you will be a good servant of Christ Jesus, constantly nourished on the words of the faith and of the sound doctrine which you have been following. (v. 6)

"Don't run from false teaching; expose it," says Paul. "Point it out. Help others identify it." Sometimes we resist exposing erroneous teaching. We don't want to come across as negative or as know-it-alls. We're afraid of offending someone. But teaching sound doctrine involves comparing it to what is false (see 1:3–4).

Notice that Paul tells Timothy to point out false doctrine to "the brethren" (v. 6a). We can't expect the world to conform to the Word. But those of us in the church have the Scriptures as our standard. And they must constantly be held up as the infallible measure of truth.

Keep Feasting on the Word

Of course, Christian leaders can't point out false doctrine if they don't maintain a steady diet of the truth themselves. That's why Paul urged Timothy to keep nourishing himself on the "words of the faith." Learning and growing don't suddenly stop with a seminary diploma. Education for Christians, especially leaders, is a lifetime endeavor.

Five Lessons for Application

Let's close with five suggestions for living out what we've learned.

1. *The present-day apostasy is a constant reminder that we are living in the "last days."* Scripture is very clear that apostasy will signal the approach of Christ's second coming. As more and more people depart from His way, we should be looking for His return.
2. *The bottom line of all lies is Satan.* Satan is the root of all false teaching. He uses people. He divides churches. He entraps teachers. He uses anything he can to advance his "doctrines of demons." We don't take Satan lightly; so let's not take his lies lightly either.
3. *Satan has his spokesmen.* Don't be taken in by charisma, success, or clever speech. Satan often appears as an "angel of

light" (2 Cor. 11:13–15), working through attractive, convincing people. Remember to measure everything against the Word, our standard.

4. *A sign of maturity is properly enjoying God's provisions, rather than refusing them.* James says that "every good thing bestowed and every perfect gift is from above" (James 1:17a). Are you enjoying what God has given you? Material possessions? Good health? Close relationships? Salvation? Sure, there may be times when we have to give up something in order to grow spiritually. But often, we just need to appreciate and enjoy what God has provided.

5. *Part of a good, nourishing ministry is exposing heresy.* Sometimes we have to be negative; we have to say "That's wrong, and here's why." Not because we're killjoys. But because we want to promote real joy. Joy that's rooted in God's truth . . . and God's Son.

It's a crazy world, indeed. But where God's Word is taught and defended, there is sanity.

 Living Insights

Doctrine. That word, for some people, conjures up all kinds of unpleasant images. Granite-faced preachers who believe that cracking a smile is tantamount to breaking a commandment. Parishioners fidgeting in rigid pews during a rigid sermon. The tormented moan of a church organ, as if it, too, were grieving over secret sins. Some would even say that the teaching of doctrine promotes piety without personality, holiness without heart, obedience without joy.

"Doctrine isn't practical," others argue. "It's just head knowledge." Theologian Loraine Boettner would disagree. Consider, for example, his discussion of the practicalities of the Trinity.

> If there were no trinity, there could be no incarnation, no objective redemption, and therefore no salvation; for there would then be no one capable of acting as Mediator between God and man. In his fallen condition man has neither the inclination nor the ability to redeem himself. All merely human works are defective and incapable of redeeming a single soul. Between the Holy God and sinful man

there is an infinite gulf; and only through One who is Deity, who takes man's nature upon Himself and suffers and dies in his stead, thus giving infinite value and dignity to that suffering and death, can man's debt be paid. Nor could a Holy Spirit who comes short of Deity apply that redemption to human souls. Hence if salvation is to be had at all it must be of divine origin. If God were only unity, but not plurality, He might be our Judge, but, so far as we can see, could not be our Saviour and sanctifier. The fact of the matter is that God is the way back to Himself, and that all of the hopes of our fallen race are centred in the truth of the Trinity.[4]

Pretty practical stuff.

Don't let doctrine scare you. God didn't give us His Word to intimidate or bore us. He gave it to reveal who He is—so we can know Him, love Him, trust Him, worship Him. And what could be more practical than that?

4. Loraine Boettner, *Studies in Theology* (Presbyterian and Reformed Publishing Company, 1947), pp. 135–136.

Chapter 12

THE DOS AND DON'TS
OF MINISTRY
1 Timothy 4:6–16

Excellence requires more than merely avoiding wrong; it demands that we also embrace right.

That applies to any worthwhile endeavor. The boxer in training must do more than stop smoking, drinking, and eating doughnuts. He must also pummel the heavy bag, skip rope, and log many bruising hours in the sparring ring.

Or consider successful business executives. They don't just minimize bad decisions; they make lots of good ones. They think ahead, research the market, take calculated risks. They make it a point to know their product and their customers inside and out.

What's true in the business and athletic worlds is also true in ministry. Sure, there are practices any minister needs to steer clear of. But we also need to pursue the *right* things with vigor and enthusiasm. Maybe this "avoid wrong/embrace right" philosophy is what Paul wanted to pass on to Timothy in 1 Timothy 4:6–16. We could call this section Paul's "dos and don'ts" of ministry. It stacks up a balanced list of positives and negatives that will help any minister maintain excellence.

A Major Goal for All in Ministry

Paul presents his list within the framework of one overall goal.

> In pointing out these things to the brethren, you will be *a good servant of Christ Jesus,* constantly nourished on the words of the faith and of the sound doctrine which you have been following. (4:6, emphasis added)

Serve in the name of Christ and to His glory—that's what ministers are to do. And all Christians are ministers, whether they preach from the pulpit, sing in the choir, or help behind the scenes. Whatever our contribution to the body, serving Christ is our goal.

Notice the marks of good servants of Christ. First, they point out truth to God's people (v. 6a), whether from the pulpit or in their lifestyle. Second, they nourish themselves on the Word of God (v. 6b), feeding others from the fullness of their souls. And third, they live what they teach (v. 6c), humbly following God's Word.

Too often, we evaluate ministers by their eloquent speech, level of education, their air of professionalism, or their busyness. But God wants to know, "Are you My servant? Has my Word penetrated your mind and heart enough that you can discern truth from error and display it for others? Are you living what you claim to believe?"

Guidelines to Follow in Pursuing the Goal

With this general framework in mind, let's examine Paul's specific dos and don'ts for serving well in ministry.

A quick read-through of the passage reveals that Paul presents his case with alternating negative and positive exhortations.

Negatively	Positively
• Have nothing to do with worldly fables (v. 7a)	• Discipline yourself for the purpose of godliness (vv. 7b–11)
• Don't feel inferior because of your youth (v. 12a)	• Live an exemplary life (v. 12b)
• Don't neglect your gift (v. 14)	• Pay close attention to yourself and your teaching (vv. 15–16)

Let's take each one individually and dig in a little deeper.

Have Nothing to Do with Worldly Fables

But have nothing to do with worldly fables fit only for old women. (v. 7a)

If we're not nourishing ourselves on God's truth, we'll be tempted to fill ourselves with something else. That's why Paul told Timothy to avoid "fables." This is the same Greek word translated as *myths* in 1:4. Commentator Philip H. Towner explains that the term

classifies material not simply as untrue or legendary but as pernicious in its (or its author's) purpose to justify immoral or improper behavior on the basis of a divine or traditional pattern. Thus grounds for certain immoral practices could be found in the behavior attributed to the gods.[1]

Paul isn't condemning the likes of *Grimm's Fairy Tales* or *Aesop's Fables*. Rather, he's warning against stories and beliefs manufactured to promote and defend an immoral lifestyle. Such stories, instead of leading hearers to moral high ground, lose them in the shifting sands of popular standards. Since myths and fables oppose God's historical acts as well as Christ's reality, Paul says, "Keep your distance from them, and feed on the truth instead."

Need a modern-day example? How about the wave of "angelmania" washing over America? Books on angels are everywhere. How to speak to your personal angels. How to tap into your angelic guide. What to do if you meet an angel during an out-of-body experience.

Such literature, though often touching and entertaining, usually ignores the biblical profile of angels and denies the reality of sin, our desperate need for God, and His sovereign management of the universe. The real danger of angelmania is that it serves as a spiritual substitute for readers. It mesmerizes them with stories of the supernatural, but diverts them from the real God and prevents them from dealing with crucial spiritual issues.

Discipline Yourself for Godliness

> On the other hand, discipline yourself for the purpose of godliness. (v. 7b)

The opposite of lending a lazy ear to fables is disciplining oneself for godliness. The Greek word for *discipline* is *gumnazo*, which means "to train." We get our word *gymnasium* from it. Paul's use of athletic imagery reminds us that spiritual growth doesn't happen by accident. It takes sweat, determination, perseverance, and total submission to the Trainer.

"*Godliness*," writes Towner, "is Paul's term in the Pastorals for 'genuine Christianity'; it brings together knowledge of and faith in God and the observable response of lifestyle."[2] You might say that godliness is taking God seriously. To reach this goal, we must be "Christians in training." And spiritual training, as Paul says in the

1. Philip H. Towner, *1–2 Timothy and Titus*, The IVP New Testament Commentary Series (Downers Grove, Ill.: InterVarsity Press, 1994), p. 45.

2. Towner, *1–2 Timothy and Titus*, p. 65.

next verse, gets us fit for eternity.

> For bodily discipline is only of little profit, but god-
> liness is profitable for all things, since it holds prom-
> ise for the present life and also for the life to come.
> It is a trustworthy statement deserving full accep-
> tance. (vv. 8–9)

Is Paul saying that we should forget about physical exercise?
Not at all. He is simply making a comparison between the temporal
benefits of physical training and the eternal benefits of spiritual
training. Pumping iron and running marathons will help keep our
bodies in shape. But spiritual disciplines—prayer, Bible study, worship, Christian service, evangelism—produce results for this life
and the next.

And like physical discipline, spiritual discipline also has a goal
in sight.

> For it is for this we labor and strive, because we have
> fixed our hope on the living God, who is the Savior
> of all men, especially of believers. Prescribe and
> teach these things. (vv. 10–11)

Godliness, remember, is our goal in the spiritual life (see v. 7b).
We "labor and strive" for it. *Strive* is the Greek word *agonizomai*;
from its root we get our word *agonize*. Becoming godly takes work—
it's a struggle. But it's not like an earthly struggle, for we draw
strength for it from our living Lord (v. 10b).

Don't Feel Inferior Because of Your Youth

> Let no one look down on your youthfulness. (v. 12a)

Why would Paul need to say this? It could be that Timothy,
realizing he was much younger than many of the people to whom
he ministered, felt that his age was a handicap. Paul quickly cor-
rected this misconception by pointing out that spiritual maturity,
not physical maturity, is the key to effective ministry.

> Don't let anyone look down on you because you
> are young: see that they look up to you because you
> are an example to believers in your speech and be-
> haviour, in your love and faith and sincerity.
> (v. 12 PHILLIPS)

"Don't worry about your age, Timothy," says Paul. "Concentrate on living an exemplary life. If people see Christ in you, they will notice Him instead of your age."

Don't Neglect Your Ministry

> Until I come, give attention to the public reading of Scripture, to exhortation and teaching. Do not neglect the spiritual gift within you, which was bestowed upon you through prophetic utterance with the laying on of hands by the presbytery. (vv. 13–14)

Once again, Paul reminds Timothy of the Word's primacy in ministry. Notice how God expects His ministers to deliver His Word. They are to read, exhort, and teach the Scriptures. Commentators Barton, Veerman, and Wilson explain these three activities.

> Timothy was to regularly do *public reading of Scripture* in his congregation, a practice begun in Old Testament times (see Exodus 24:7; Deuteronomy 31:11; Joshua 8:35; 2 Kings 23:2–3; Nehemiah 8:1–18) and continued in the synagogues (Luke 4:16; Acts 15:21; Colossians 4:16; 1 Thessalonians 5:27).
> *Teaching* refers to training in Christian doctrine. The people needed to know, understand, and constantly be reminded of the great truths of the Christian faith.
> *Preaching* could also be translated "exhortation." In addition to reading the Scripture, Timothy was to exhort, that is, to warn, advise, and urge his listeners regarding the words of Scripture, helping them apply those words to their daily lives.[3]

God didn't intend for His Word to be skimmed over lightly. He wants it to penetrate our ears, our minds, our hearts—every thread in the fabric of our lives. That's why solid preaching and individual study of the Word are so important (see Neh. 8:1–8, 12–18). We don't absorb God's truth by gliding over it. We must immerse ourselves in it, explore its depths, take in its wonder.

For Timothy to deliver the Word powerfully and effectively, it

---

3. Bruce B. Barton, David R. Veerman, Neil Wilson, *1 Timothy, 2 Timothy, Titus*, Life Application Bible Commentary series (Wheaton, Ill.: Tyndale House Publishers, 1993), p. 89.

meant using the "spiritual gift" given to him at his ordination (1 Tim. 4:14). The Holy Spirit gives us all gifts to use to the glory of God. If we neglect to use them, we minister in our own strength and deprive others of seeing God work through us.

Pay Close Attention to Yourself and to Your Teaching

> Take pains with these things; be absorbed in them, so that your progress may be evident to all. Pay close attention to yourself and to your teaching; persevere in these things; for as you do this you will insure salvation both for yourself and for those who hear you. (vv. 15–16)

Paul closes this section with a final positive exhortation. Notice the words he uses to encourage Timothy to spiritual excellence: "Take pains" (v. 15); "be absorbed" (v. 15); "pay close attention to" (v. 16). These are all words of deliberate action. "Concentrate on your personal spiritual development and your teaching of the Word, Timothy," says Paul, "and two things will happen: you'll insure salvation for yourself and others."

Wait a minute. Is Paul saying we can be saved by something besides grace? Philip Towner helps us understand Paul's promise.

> [Salvation] signifies a process of development that begins with belief in Christ (conversion) and the gift of new life in the Spirit (regeneration) and will end (our glorification) with the return of Christ. In this life we experience the process of salvation as stages of growth in "Christlikeness," "putting on the new self" (Col 3:11), working out our salvation (Phil 2:12); and many things can impede growth. Essential to growth, however, is the ministry of God's Word in preaching and teaching in the church.[4]

Lasting Lessons Worth Remembering

What general life lessons can we take from Paul's specific instructions to Timothy? How about these five for starters.

1. *There is no higher goal in ministry than servanthood.* Our first and foremost priority is to be a "good servant of Christ Jesus" (v. 6).

4. Towner, *1–2 Timothy and Titus*, p. 113.

Servanthood shouldn't decrease with authority or position; it should increase (consider Christ's example in Matt. 20:25–28).

2. *There is no greater temptation in ministry than extremism.* In this 1 Timothy passage, notice, there is balance. Paul urges both devotion and discipline, public service and private integrity, teaching others and learning and growing personally. Those who exhort other people must first examine themselves. They must avoid untruth while actively pursuing truth. A biblical, healthy ministry doesn't go overboard in certain areas but strives to maintain a balanced approach.

3. *There is no more effective style of ministry than biblical exposition.* God has entrusted His Word to us, which is rich in nourishment for the soul. We must feast on it first, then read it to others, explain it, and help them apply it.

4. *There is no better formula for a growing ministry than a growing minister.* Notice verse 12, "Show yourself an example," and verse 15, "So that your progress may be evident to all." You want your ministry to grow, to deepen, to move with the flow of God's hand? Start with yourself.

5. *There is no better proof of a ministry's authenticity than perseverance.* "Persevere in these things," says Paul (v. 16). Ministries that stay with the task over the long haul will reach the lost, nurture new Christians, and deepen all believers. So if you want to know where God's working, don't look for flashy buildings or frantic pastors. Don't even look for the biggest crowds. Look for men and women who take God seriously and strive to please Him during good times and bad.

 Living Insights

"Discipline yourself for the purpose of godliness," Paul told Timothy (4:7). How does the apostle's exhortation hit you? Does it stir up your soul to love Christ more deeply, serve Him more faithfully? Or does the command clank around in your ear like the heavy chains of legalism? Does *spiritual discipline* strike you as a contradictory phrase? Should planning, consistency—even hard work—have any part in the lives of those saved purely by God's grace? As Kent Hughes says in his book *Disciplines of a Godly Man*, we need to understand the difference between discipline and legalism.

Underlying much of the conscious rejection of spiritual discipline is the fear of legalism. For many, spiritual discipline means putting oneself back under the Law with a series of Draconian rules which no one can live up to—and which spawn frustration and spiritual death.

But nothing could be farther from the truth if you understand what discipline and legalism are. The difference is one of *motivation*: legalism is self-centered; discipline is God-centered. The legalistic heart says, "I will do this thing to gain merit with God." The disciplined heart says, "I will do this thing because I love God and want to please Him." There is an infinite difference between the *motivation* of legalism and discipline! Paul knew this implicitly and fought the legalists bare-knuckled all the way across Asia Minor, never giving an inch. And now he shouts to us, "Train [discipline] yourself to be godly"! If we confuse legalism and discipline, we do so to our soul's peril.[5]

Do you feel you're running the spiritual race with vigor, enthusiasm, and perseverance? Or do you feel spiritually slow, sluggish, and apathetic?

_____

_____

What adjustments can you make in your lifestyle that will help you become a more disciplined believer and, at the same time, keep you free from the chains of legalism? For example, you could

♦ reach for the Bible instead of the TV remote control more often;

♦ trade some busyness for more reflective time with God;

♦ interact more about spiritual things with your spouse, children, or friends.

_____

5. R. Kent Hughes, *Disciplines of a Godly Man* (Wheaton, Ill.: Good News Publishers, Crossway Books, 1991), p. 17.

_____

_____

_____

Go ahead. Work up a good spiritual sweat. It's healthier for your heart than you might think.

Chapter 13

RESPECTING AND REBUKING THE SAINTS

1 Timothy 5:1–3, 17–20

I love the ministry . . . it's the people I can't stand!"

At some point in his ministry, every pastor makes such a declaration, quickly followed by a chuckle he hopes will vent some of the pressure that comes from trying to meet the needs of his flock. Even in jest, though, that statement reflects the gravity of the minister's task. Ministry is tough, because we live in a sinful world inhabited by sinful people. Eugene Peterson describes the minister's challenge this way:

> Sundays are easy. The sanctuary is clean and orderly, the symbolism clear, the people polite. I know what I am doing: I am going to lead this people in worship, proclaim God's word to them, celebrate the sacraments. I have had time to prepare my words and spirit. And the people are ready, arriving dressed up and expectant. Centuries of tradition converge in this Sunday singing of hymns, exposition of Scripture, commitments of faith, offering of prayers, baptizing, eating and drinking the life of our Lord. I love doing this. I wake up early Sunday mornings, the adrenaline pumping into my veins.
>
> But after the sun goes down on Sundays, the clarity diffuses. From Monday through Saturday, an unaccountably unruly people track mud through the holy places, leaving a mess. The order of worship gives way to the disorder of argument and doubt, bodies in pain and emotions in confusion, misbehaving children and misdirected parents. . . . The vision of myself as pastor, so clear in Lord's Day worship, is now blurred and distorted as it is reflected back from the eyes of people who view me as pawn to their egos. The affirmations I experience in Sunday greetings are now precarious in the slippery mud of put-down and fault-finding.[1]

1. Eugene H. Peterson, *The Contemplative Pastor: Returning to the Art of Spiritual Direction* (Grand Rapids, Mich.: William B. Eerdmans Publishing Co., 1989), pp. 53–54.

The truth is that none of us, including pastors, are perfect. If a church has people, that church has problems. This has always been true. That's why Paul gave Timothy thorough instructions on how to minister among a fellowship of flawed saints.

A General Glance at 1 Timothy 5

Up to this point, Paul has had a lot to say about doctrine and important issues related to the function of the church. But in the fifth chapter of 1 Timothy, Paul focuses on the specific needs of particular groups of people within the church.

- In verses 1–2, he explains how to admonish men and women of various ages.

- In verses 3–16, he describes how to honor and provide for widows.

- In verses 17–18, he instructs how to doubly honor elders who are worthy.

- In verses 19–20, he explains how to rebuke elders who are sinning.

- In verses 21–25, he provides personal counsel to Timothy.

The body of Christ contains people of all ages, abilities, and levels of maturity. Paul's instructions to Timothy in this chapter suggest that being aware of this diversity will help us respect and, when necessary, rebuke the saints in a way that glorifies God and strengthens the church.

A Specific Study of Congregational Needs

A minister must sometimes approach members of his congregation for the purpose of correction. When he does, he must consider closely not only what he's going to say and how he's going to say it but *to whom* he will be speaking. Let's look, then, at God's instructions for approaching various members of His household.

Older Men

Do not sharply rebuke an older man, but rather appeal to him as a father. (v. 1a)

The word for *older man* here is *presbuteros*, which means "elder."

Paul, however, isn't using the term in this context to describe the office of elder but an older man.[2]

To "sharply rebuke" (*epiplesso*) these older men, to admonish them harshly or abrasively, would have been disrespectful.[3] Rather, Paul says to "appeal to" (*parakaleo*) an older man as a father. This is a softer word, suggesting concern and personal involvement.[4] When correcting older people, we want to preserve their dignity and worth.

An older person has lived more of life than we have. So, though we don't compromise the Word or condone sin, we speak with love, respect, and gentleness, as to a father.

All this begs the question, "Is it ever right to rebuke a member of the church?" Yes it is, according to 2 Timothy 4:2.

> Preach the word; be ready in season and out of season; reprove, *rebuke*, exhort, with great patience and instruction. (emphasis added)

Sometimes God's Word must be used to rebuke members of the church. But the Greek word in 2 Timothy is *epitimao*, not *epiplesso*. It means "to mete out due measure." So the question is not whether to rebuke, but when and how. And where older men are concerned, it must be done gently.

Younger Men

> Appeal to . . . the younger men as brothers. (1 Tim. 5:1b)

We're not to be offensive or needlessly abrasive with younger men either, but we don't have to approach them as gingerly as we would older men. With brothers, we can be more direct and to the point than with fathers. We appeal to them as equals and peers, remembering that their good and God's glory are our goals.

Older Women

> [Appeal to] the older women as mothers. (v. 2a)

---

2. Philip H. Towner, *1–2 Timothy and Titus*, The IVP New Testament Commentary Series (Downers Grove, Ill.: InterVarsity Press, 1994), p. 115.

3. The Greek word translated *sharply rebuke* (*epiplesso*) literally means "to strike at." It carries overtones of violent treatment.

4. Towner, *1–2 Timothy and Titus*, pp. 114–15.

Older women, too, must be handled with special consideration —with the same tenderness, respect, love, and honor that we would show our own mothers. Again, this doesn't prohibit direct communication, nor does it condone compromising the Word. But correction must be applied with compassion.

Younger Women

> [Appeal to] the younger women as sisters, in all purity. (v. 2b)

How should a brother treat his little sister? He should treat her gently, recognizing that she bruises easier than his rowdy friends at the schoolyard. He should protect her, respect her, set an example for her. And he should keep his relationship with her pure, avoiding any sensuality or immorality that will cause her to compromise her integrity.

Father, brother, mother, sister. These are family terms. *Coworker, boss, underling,* and *employee* are nowhere to be found in this passage. Paul's point seems clear enough—the church is not a corporation; it's a family. A family whose members need each other and should approach one another with the love modeled by our heavenly Father.

Widows

Paul gives considerable attention to dealing sensitively and responsibly with those who have lost their mates. So rather than rush through this section, we'll devote our entire next chapter to the special needs of widows.

Worthy Elders

In verse 17, Paul addresses the welfare of those who serve as elders.

> Let the elders who rule well be considered worthy of double honor, especially those who work hard at preaching and teaching. For the Scripture says, "You shall not muzzle the ox while he is threshing," and "The laborer is worthy of his wages."
> (vv. 17–18)

Paul obviously has the office of elder in mind here. And he specifically focuses on two groups: "elders who rule well" and "those who work hard at preaching and teaching." The first group seems to refer to those elders who excel in the ministry of leadership. In today's culture, they would probably be full-time staff pastors. The second, most likely, is a subgroup of the first and consists of those elders who add preaching and teaching to their leadership responsibilities. Paul seems to draw some distinction between those on the "elder board" and the senior pastor.

These two classes of elders, especially those who preach and teach, are worthy of "double honor." Verse 18 is the key to unlocking that phrase. In that verse, Paul quotes Deuteronomy 25:4 and applies it to a pastor's income and the congregation's responsibility to support him (see also 1 Cor. 9:3–18). Commentators Barton, Veerman, and Wilson explain:

> Often oxen were used to tread out the grain on a threshing floor. The animal was attached by poles to a large millstone. As it walked around the millstone, its hooves trampled the grain, separating the kernels from the chaff. At the same time, the millstone ground the grain into flour. Muzzling the ox would prevent it from eating while it was working. Paul used this illustration to argue that productive Christian workers should receive financial support. The fact that a person is in Christian ministry doesn't mean that he or she should be poorly paid.[5]

And all the preachers said, "Amen!"

There's no need, however, to limit the "double honor" principle to money. Christian leaders should also be paid high respect, honor, and appreciation by those they serve.

Sinning Elders

> Do not receive an accusation against an elder except on the basis of two or three witnesses. Those who continue in sin, rebuke in the presence of all, so that the rest also may be fearful of sinning. (1 Tim. 5:19–20)

Even elders err. And some may even engage in sinful behavior. If so, proper confrontation is in order. So Paul draws on an Old

5. Bruce B. Barton, David R. Veerman, and Neil Wilson, *1 Timothy, 2 Timothy, Titus*, Life Application Bible Commentary Series (Wheaton, Ill.: Tyndale House Publishers, 1993), p. 108.

Testament principle requiring that the sin be confirmed by two or three witnesses (Deut. 19:15). Why? To weed out groundless rumors and malicious confrontation. Elders and pastors can be unpopular with the congregation for many reasons—sometimes for preaching the truth. So before action can be taken against a leader, there must be sufficient and reliable evidence against him. Gossip is no grounds for rebuking an elder or any other believer.

What if an elder, or any other church member, persists in sin after being properly confronted? That's where church discipline comes in. First Timothy 5:20 highlights the public exposure of sin, but that's not the first stage of discipline. Jesus stresses the importance of first approaching the individual in private to resolve the problem (see Matt. 18:15–17).

Church discipline is an unpleasant but necessary part of the ministry. It's God's prescription for restoring wayward sheep, maintaining holiness in the flock, and warning the church of sin's destructive power. But let's take care to not develop a Gestapo mentality, always looking for someone to slip up so we can bring down the hammer.

Here are some other thoughts to help apply church discipline in a godly manner.

1. *Even though others may be living a sinful lifestyle, that doesn't give us the right to bully or despise them.* Uncontrolled anger, pride, haste, and self-righteousness have no place in church discipline. How can we restore others to Christlikeness if we're not Christlike?

2. *There is a place in the church for personal rebuke and discipline, when it's performed scripturally.* Remember, the purpose of church discipline is purity and restoration, not vengeance. Discipline in the hands of the unwise or biblically illiterate is like a loaded gun in the hands of a child.

3. *The greatest judgment we are to perform is judgment on ourselves.* Jesus said, "First take the log out of your own eye, and then you will see clearly to take the speck out of your brother's eye" (Matt. 7:5). We need to take a good look at ourselves before we come down hard on someone else (see also 1 Cor. 11:31; Gal. 6:1).

One of the most difficult jobs facing any pastor is the challenge of disciplining and correcting the saints. Handled properly though, even a rebuke will maintain the respect and honor due our brothers and sisters in Christ.

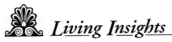 *Living Insights*

Take some time to consider whether you're extending "double honor" to your pastor. The following questions will help.

How do you view your pastor? As an employee who must answer to a congregation full of bosses? Or a shepherd sent by the Great Shepherd to protect, feed, and lead His sheep?

_____

_____

Make a list—an honest one—of the expectations you place on your pastor.

_____

_____

_____

_____

Are these expectations realistic? Do they hold him to a high standard of character without demanding perfection? Do they match the real needs of the congregation or just the wants? Do they take into account the pastor's schedule, his abilities, and the priorities laid out in Scripture?

_____

_____

_____

_____

Do you know your pastor's salary? Is it commensurate with the demands of the job, the area in which he lives, the size of his family, and the income of the rest of the congregation?

_____

How do you respond when the pastor does something you think is wrong? Do you closely evaluate whether the problem is worth addressing? Or do you want to "fix it" right away? Do you allow the pastor room to grow, just like you need room to grow? Have you ever approached the pastor personally about some of your concerns? Or is gossip more your style?

_____

_____

_____

_____

_____

What can you do this week to honor your pastor, elders, or other leaders of the congregation?

_____

_____

_____

_____

_____

 ## Digging Deeper

When you pray for a minister and how he relates to his flock, you might want to remember the special battles he faces. He, as well as you, would like to see victory in the following areas.

Special Battles of the Minister

1. Authoritarianism—needlessly repressing the freedom of God's people; becoming inflexible, dictatorial, unteachable, and

proud. This is leadership gone wild, and a pastor like this needs to be reproved.

2. Exclusiveness—promoting a clannish, cliquish kind of following; harboring an attitude of "I alone am right" or "We alone are right." Paranoia often accompanies this kind of mentality, "The people out there are against us!"

3. Greed—hungering for money; performing ministry (for example, weddings, funerals, etc.) for the money in it. Some sure advice for a pastor is to not be involved in the collection of the church's money.

4. Rationalization—justifying wrong with a defensive spirit; quickly glossing over inappropriate actions. A pastor who rationalizes will often twist scriptural truth to fit his lifestyle.

5. Sensuality—partaking in a lifestyle of sexual looseness; being too familiar with the opposite sex. If a leader is going to claim God's hand on his life, then he must stay away from moral compromise.

6. Unaccountability—being secretive, irresponsible, or untouchable. Beware of men who hide behind the statement, "I am God's anointed." No matter how eloquent or competent a pastor is, he still needs to accept the loving confrontation of friends.

Chapter 14

WHAT ABOUT WIDOWS?

1 Timothy 5:3–16

W e're not told how he died. But when he died, he owed money.
And his poor widow inherited the debt. So the creditors
had come to collect her only valuables—her two sons. Whatever
price the boys would fetch at the slave market would be used to
balance the books. Then the widow would be free of debt . . .
but imprisoned in a dungeon of loneliness and grief, wondering if
she would ever see her sons again.

In desperation, she sought help from the man of God.

"What else do you have in the house?" the prophet Elisha asked
the widow.

"Nothing but a jar of oil."

"Go, collect all the empty vessels you can find," he said. "And
fill them all from the one jar you have."

So the woman and her sons blanketed the neighborhood and
borrowed every pot, jar, and bowl not in use at that moment. They
lined them all up; then they poured . . . and poured . . . and
poured. Until every container was brimming with oil.

"Now go sell the oil," said the prophet.

The widow used the proceeds to pay off her husband's debt and
still had enough to feed her family—a family of three.

Throughout Scripture, God reveals that He has a special place in
His heart for widows, as this story from 2 Kings 4:1–7 affirms. And
He holds those accountable who neglect or take advantage of them
(see Exod. 22:22–24; Deut. 10:17–18; 14:28–29; 24:17–22; Ps. 146:9;
Prov. 15:25; Isa. 1:17; Jer. 7:6–7; Zech. 7:8–10; Mal. 3:5; James
1:27). Clearly, He wants the vulnerable and defenseless protected.

Shouldn't the church, then, extend the care and compassion
toward widows that God expects of us? Indeed. But sometimes
congregations get distracted by other activities and forget to take
care of those who can't care for themselves. Or they go to the other
extreme and let their emotions disallow healthy discernment, giving
to those less needy and thus depriving those truly in need. So Paul
offers some sound advice to help us attentively and wisely care for
the special needs of widows.

Observations Regarding Widows

You won't find a heftier chunk of Scripture devoted to the topic of widows than 1 Timothy 5:3–16. In order to take in all Paul has to say here, let's first get a general overview of the passage, then we'll delve into the specifics.

General Categories of Widows

Paul appears to have in mind four groups of women who have lost their mates.

Widows indeed (vv. 3, 5, 16b). These women are desolate, without means of support or relatives to assist them.

Widows who have living relatives (vv. 4, 8, 16a). These widows have children, grandchildren, or other relatives who can help support them.

Widows who live carnal lives (vv. 6, 11–13, 15). These women, rather than using their new position in life to worship God and serve the saints with undistracted devotion, are living a loose lifestyle.

Widows who are "on the list" (vv. 9–10). Apparently, churches in Timothy's day were to keep a registry of widows who qualified for financial support from the church. Some widows were to be kept on the list, others excluded.

Financial Support of Widows

It may strike us as unusual that Paul would devote so much ink to the proper care of widows. But consider the day in which he and Timothy ministered. Many men were ostracized, persecuted, and even put to death for following the new Christian faith—leaving their wives, some of them very young, to fend for themselves. Women didn't have the choice of careers they have today, and there was no pension plan or Social Security for them to depend on. The church simply had to have some kind of plan for the care of these special women.

Whom Should the Church Support?

Paul, however, doesn't promote an indiscriminate distribution of funds. Rather, he counsels Timothy to first determine which widows qualify for support and which ones do not.

Widows Indeed

"Honor widows who are widows indeed," Paul says (v. 3). *Honor* is a revealing word, especially for those who might accuse Paul of being hard on women. The Greek word used here is the verb form of the word Paul uses in verse 17 in regard to elders ("double honor"). Because of that link, it has financial implications; yet it goes beyond mere material provision. The New International Version translates the verb "Give proper recognition to." The church is to treat widows with respect, dignity, and worth, not pitch them aside like a worn out shoe (compare this same word *honor* in Matt. 15:4–6; John 5:23; 1 Pet. 2:17).

Just who is a "widow indeed"? She's a widow who, first of all, has no living relatives to support her.

> If any widow has children or grandchildren, let them first learn to practice piety in regard to their own family, and to make some return to their parents; for this is acceptable in the sight of God. (1 Tim. 5:4)

In Timothy's day, when the primary breadwinner died, the responsibility for the widow's care fell to her immediate family. Perhaps some of the believers in Ephesus were avoiding their obligation to support their widowed mothers and grandmothers. Such avoidance was unbecoming to the church—a place meant to radiate active love. Maybe that's why Paul uses such strong language when he says,

> But if anyone does not provide for his own, and especially for those of his household, he has denied the faith, and is worse than an unbeliever. (v. 8)

This verse is sometimes used to exhort fathers and mothers to properly provide for their children. But the context has in view families who must go beyond that and provide for their widowed mothers and grandmothers as well. Only when a widow is without a family to sustain her should she be able to depend on the church— her larger "family"—for help.

There's also a spiritual requirement for being classified as a "widow indeed."

> Now she who is a widow indeed, and who has been left alone has fixed her hope on God, and continues in entreaties and prayers night and day. But she who gives herself to wanton pleasure is dead even while she lives. (vv. 5–6)

The church is to support widows who demonstrate a preoccupation with the things of God rather than a promiscuous lifestyle. Otherwise, the church would be contributing to the spiritual harm of one of its own. For this reason, Paul urges Timothy to deal straightforwardly and not hedge about saying such hard things:

> Prescribe these things as well, so that they may be above reproach. (v. 7)

A "widow indeed," then, has no relatives to support her, and she lives an honorable, godly life.

Widows on the List

Apparently, the early churches kept a register of all the widows who were to receive financial support. In the next few verses, Paul goes into great detail to designate those who qualify. His criteria may come across as arbitrary or exclusive. But remember, the needs of the church were overwhelming during this period of history. Simply tossing money at every problem would have been poor stewardship. Paul's guidelines remind us that we don't have to abandon wisdom and discernment in order to exercise compassion.

> Let a widow be put on the list only if she is not less than sixty years old, having been the wife of one man. (v. 9)

First, to be on the list, a widow had to be at least sixty years old, for reasons Paul gives later. Also, if she had been faithful to her husband during marriage, she was to be included. Without this requirement, a woman could live promiscuously for years, running around on her husband, then quickly join the church for support upon his death.

Instead of irresponsibility and unbridled pleasure, her life should be characterized by godly service. As J. B. Phillips renders Paul's thoughts:

> Widows for your church list should . . . have a well-founded reputation for having lived a good life. Some such questions as these should be asked:—has she brought up her children well, has she been hospitable to strangers, has she been willing to serve fellow-Christians in menial ways, has she relieved those in distress, has she, in a word, conscientiously done all the good she can? (v. 10)

Interestingly, these requirements, as Philip H. Towner notes,

> are very similar in tone, content and purpose to those
> that appear in 3:2–7 in reference to the overseer;
> they begin within the home and move outward.[1]

Exemplary Christian living—that's what it takes to make it on the list. Paul included an age requirement (sixty or older) because the younger widows tended to allow their focus to drift off of Christ.

> But refuse to put younger widows on the list, for
> when they feel sensual desires in disregard of Christ,
> they want to get married, thus incurring condemna-
> tion, because they have set aside their previous
> pledge. (vv. 11–12)

Is remarrying after the death of a mate sinful—something that will incur "condemnation"? Not at all. Paul's use of the word *pledge* (v. 12) suggests that widows in that day might have regularly made pledges to concentrate on serving the church after the death of their husbands. Since younger widows were more likely to remarry and have children than older widows, their chances of being dis-tracted from wholehearted devotion to Christ were greater. So if a younger widow were put on the list for support and then remarried, she would in effect be breaking her pledge.

Paul cites another reason to keep younger widows off the list.

> And at the same time they also learn to be idle, as
> they go around from house to house; and not merely
> idle, but also gossips and busybodies, talking about
> things not proper to mention. (v. 13)

Is Paul being unreasonably harsh on young widows? Once again, Philip Towner provides some background that sheds light on Paul's prohibition.

> [This verse] may mean that young widows, their
> financial burden lifted, lacking the spiritual maturity
> to apply themselves to prayer and other tasks of
> ministry associated with the *list*, became lazy and
> even counterproductive. But a glance down to verse

---

1. Philip H. Towner, *1–2 Timothy and Titus*, The IVP New Testament Commentary Series (Downers Grove, Ill.: InterVarsity Press, 1994), p. 117.

> 15 (*some have in fact already turned away to follow Satan*) suggests that Paul already has those young widows who had fallen prey to the false teachers in view. If so, then the gossip and other foolishness belong to the category of meaningless, paradoxical chatter (1:6; 4:7; 6:20) spread by the heretics, which Paul calls "false." It is also well to keep in mind that the false teachers were particularly effective in the homes of believers (2 Tim 3:6; Tit 1:11).[2]

So, with this kind of temptation stalking younger widows, what's the solution?

> Therefore, I want younger widows to get married, bear children, keep house, and give the enemy no occasion for reproach; for some have already turned aside to follow Satan. (vv. 14–15)

When you're pouring your life into raising a family and tending to a household, it's amazing how little time you have to waste. If idle hands are the devil's workshop, then busy hands are God's tool kit. And that's true for men as well as women.

Let's read this passage again in a more contemporary rendering:

> Don't put young widows on this list. No sooner will they get on than they'll want to get off, obsessed with wanting to get a husband rather than serving Christ in this way. By breaking their word, they're liable to go from bad to worse, frittering away their days on empty talk, gossip, and trivialities. No, I'd rather the young widows go ahead and get married in the first place, have children, manage their homes, and not give critics any foothold for finding fault. Some of them have already left and gone after Satan.[3] (vv. 11–15)

Now a final reminder that families, not the church, are the first line of support for widows.

> If any woman who is a believer has dependent widows,

2. Towner, *1–2 Timothy and Titus*, pp. 121–22.

3. Eugene H. Peterson, *The Message: The New Testament in Contemporary English* (Colorado Springs, Colo.: NavPress, 1993), p. 443.

let her assist them, and let not the church be burdened,
so that it may assist those who are widows indeed.
(v. 16)

Paul's specific mention here of women who care for widows suggests that much of their daily care depended on the woman of the family, who tended the home.

A Few Matters Worth a Second Glance

As we wrap up this lesson, let's not forget these important truths.

1. *Caring for one's dependent parents is a serious, scriptural responsibility.* Scripture commands parents to provide for their children (see Prov. 19:14; 2 Cor. 12:14b). But there comes a time when the tables turn. When the children are grown and making their own way, they're to care for their parents when their parents can no longer care for themselves.

2. *Grief doesn't always result in godliness.* Don't assume that the loss of one's mate will automatically draw a person closer to God. Sometimes the survivor will get angry with God and pull away from Him. Often, the lack of physical and emotional intimacy left by the loss will drive a widow to fulfill those needs in worldly, instead of godly, ways. Widows—and all those suffering a loss—need their brothers and sisters in Christ to not only grieve with them but provide spiritual strength, encouragement, and accountability.

3. *The church is never expected to support everyone in need.* The ministry of compassion and care must be accompanied by discernment and wisdom. What kind of stewards of the Lord's resources would we be if we indiscriminately handed out money to every need that came up without first evaluating its legitimacy?

4. *A full, busy life is much safer than an idle one.* Serving the Lord, studying His Word, raising a family, earning an income, building quality relationships. When we spend our time on these endeavors, we'll be less likely to fill the empty hours with frivolous or harmful activities.

Caring for widows—and all the needy in God's family—isn't optional; it's essential. And when we do it, we imitate Him who is a husband to the widow, a father to the orphan, and a provider for the poor.

✿ *Living Insights*

In his commentary on 1 Timothy, Philip H. Towner closes out this section on widows with a charge to the modern church. If you don't mind being challenged, consider what he has to say.

> Our technological age is creating some problems (or at least raising them to proportions never before known). . . . What about our poor—the homeless, the jobless? What about our disfranchised—the single mothers, the elderly, the convicts and ex-convicts, the divorced? While the questions come easier than the answers, I think we will all agree that the church is to be God's channel of compassion as he seeks to include the excluded. Paul's treatment suggests that there is far more involved than simply handing out money. The pattern presented here is a carefully structured ministry to the whole person which encourages and facilitates godliness and a productive life while it also guards against misuse and abuse that might endanger the church's witness. It remains for us to implement this teaching creatively in our particular situations.[4]

What is your "particular situation"? Do you believe that your church is ministering adequately to widows and others who need special care?

_____

_____

_____

What groups, if any, are being neglected?

_____

_____

_____

4. Towner, *1–2 Timothy and Titus*, p. 123.

How can you help make ministering to the needy a more deliberate and planned activity for your church and for yourself? How about inviting a widow, divorcee, or someone who's homeless over for the holidays? Do you know a lot about job hunting—how to prepare a résumé, build a network, prepare for an interview? Someone who's out of work might benefit from your expertise. Do you have some skills you could impart to a young person to make him or her more employable in the summer job market? What about hiring someone to work for you? Or tutoring someone whose lack of education is a hindrance to finding work? What else?

Chapter 15

A PRESCRIPTION FOR
PASTORAL HEALTH

1 Timothy 5:21–25

The Word of God keeps us spiritually healthy in a variety of ways. On Sunday mornings it bubbles out from the pulpit like a hot spring and soothes our aching souls. During personal study and reflection, it exercises our spiritual muscles and gives us strength for the day. But sometimes we need an injection—a stout dose of biblical advice delivered by a firm but loving friend. Oh, it may sting at first, especially if we're used to prescribing our own treatment or being doctored from a distance. But a well-placed challenge, admonition, or encouraging word from a Christian brother or sister can keep us on the road to spiritual health and keep us out of the infirmary.

In 1 Timothy 5:21–25, Paul supplements his steady teaching on the church with a personal message to Timothy. By pricking his protégé with a loving challenge, the apostle not only shores up Timothy's spiritual health but the health of the believers under his care.

And it's good medicine for us too.

An Overall Health Plan

Paul's prescription aims to cure several sore spots.

Partiality (v. 21). Giving preferential treatment to certain members of the congregation or fostering a bias against others can make the whole body ill. Paul recommends objectivity to treat it.

Choosing leaders hastily (v. 22a). If church leaders do not meet set spiritual criteria (see 3:1–13), a congregation can be wracked with untold suffering. Discernment and time to determine a candidate's character are Paul's preventive medicines.

Sin (5:22b, 24–25). By impulsively choosing, we share a part in the responsibility for sins committed by unqualified leaders. An excellent ministry is one that's sensitive to the possibility of sin.

Physical ailments (v. 23). Paul even includes Timothy's physical health in his prescription. Taking a little wine for stomach ailments, though, requires self-control.

A Closer Look at the Cure

Now that we know the conditions Paul wants to remedy, let's look at some of the specifics involved in treating them.

Partiality

Having urged Timothy to publicly rebuke elders who continue in sin (v. 20), Paul now reminds Timothy that such confrontation, and all ministry, must function without any preferential treatment.

> I solemnly charge you in the presence of God and of Christ Jesus and of His chosen angels, to maintain these principles without bias, doing nothing in a spirit of partiality. (v. 21)

If we play favorites in ministry, we do so before the watchful gaze of God, Christ, and the heavenly host. Quite an incentive for fairness.

The Greek word for *bias* could be translated *prejudgment*,[1] while *partiality* carries the idea of having inclination toward one rather than toward another.[2] Both are serious temptations for all of us, as commentators Barton, Veerman, and Wilson explain.

> We must be constantly on guard against favoritism, against giving preferential treatment to some and ignoring others. We live in a society that plays favorites. It's easy to give special treatment to those who are gifted, intelligent, rich, or beautiful without realizing what we are doing. We can also fall into the trap of deliberately working against people we happen not to like. The impartiality that Paul insisted on goes both ways: for example, we are neither to undermine those with whom we have a superficial disagreement, nor are we to overlook false teaching or sexual improprieties of a pastor who happens to be a dynamic speaker. Make sure that you honor people for who they are in Christ, not for who they are in the world.[3]

1. *NASB-NIV Parallel New Testament in Greek and English,* trans. Alfred Marshall (Grand Rapids, Mich.: Zondervan Publishing House, Regency Reference Library, 1986), p. 609.

2. Donald Guthrie, *The Pastoral Epistles: An Introduction and Commentary,* 2d ed. (Grand Rapids, Mich.: William B. Eerdmans Publishing Co., 1990), p. 119.

3. Bruce B. Barton, David R. Veerman, and Neil Wilson, *1 Timothy, 2 Timothy, Titus,* Life Application Bible Commentary series (Wheaton, Ill.: Tyndale House Publishers, 1993), p. 111.

Ministry, like justice, is blind. We must minister to all individuals in the body as equals in Christ.

Choosing Leaders Hastily

Partiality can cause churches to select leaders on the basis of popularity or charisma instead of character. No wonder Paul warned Timothy,

> Do not lay hands upon anyone too hastily and thus share responsibility for the sins of others. (v. 22a)

To "lay hands upon" someone was to publicly identify and authorize that person as a leader (see also 4:14; Acts 13:3).[4] This was no light or merely traditional act but one which assured the people that this leader's life had been thoroughly examined and he was worthy of their trust. It was like putting the church's seal of approval on him.

How does your church select elders and deacons? Do parishioners give careful consideration to the character of those they recommend? Or do they base their decisions on a hurried announcement and a flurry of forms distributed at the end of the morning service?

If we select leaders haphazardly and put unqualified people in charge, we share responsibility for their sins. Commentators Barton, Veerman, and Wilson elaborate.

> Anyone who took part in ordaining an elder who later proved to be unfit for the position shared in the blame for negative effects on the church. If Timothy ordained a man who became a liability because of his persistent sinning, and if Timothy allowed that man to remain in the office despite those sins, Timothy would actually *participate in* those sins by compromising himself.[5]

God takes the selection of leaders seriously, and so should we.

Sin

Rather than risk sharing in someone's sin, Paul tells Timothy,

---

4. Besides ordaining new leaders, Paul may have had in mind the reinstatement of leaders who had wandered into sin. In either case, hasty decisions can be disastrous.

5. Barton, Veerman, and Wilson, *1 Timothy, 2 Timothy, Titus*, p. 111.

Keep yourself free from sin. . . . The sins of some men are quite evident, going before them to judgment; for others, their sins follow after. Likewise also, deeds that are good are quite evident, and those which are otherwise cannot be concealed. (vv. 22b, 24–25)

These "sins" are apparently the sins of unqualified leaders referred to in verse 22a. Duane Litfin sews together these two patches of Scripture for us.

All people are heading toward judgment, carrying with them either their sins or their good works. For some, their sins or good works go before them and are obvious to all observers. For others their sins or good works trail behind, hidden from view, becoming known only after the individual has passed. Thus Paul emphasized the difficulties inherent in choosing qualified candidates for the ordination. Hasty, superficial assessments, whether positive or negative, are sometimes inaccurate, leading to the enlistment of unqualified men or the overlooking of those whose fine qualities are less obvious. With time, however, a man's true colors will emerge to an astute observer. Thus the perceptive observations of verses 24–25 are designed to underline the warning of verse 22: do not rush to ordain someone.[6]

Physical Ailments

From the spiritual health of the church, Paul shifts to the physical health of Timothy.

No longer drink water exclusively, but use a little wine for the sake of your stomach and your frequent ailments. (v. 23)

It appears that Timothy was often ill, and that he might have thought or been told that treatment was unspiritual (compare

6. A. Duane Litfin, "1 Timothy," in *The Bible Knowledge Commentary*, New Testament edition, ed. John F. Walvoord and Roy B. Zuck (Wheaton, Ill.: Scripture Press Publications, Victor Books, 1983), p. 745.

4:3–5; Col. 2:16–23). So Paul counters this heretical quackery and encourages Timothy to go ahead and take a little wine for relief.

A couple of insights emerge from this verse. First, Paul is recommending "a little" wine for *medicinal* purposes. Since the science of medicine was in its infancy in Timothy's day, people used wine as a remedy for certain ailments. The use of this verse to justify heavy or habitual drinking is irresponsible interpretation. W. C. Fields tried that approach when he said, "I only keep a bottle around in case of snakebites. I also keep a small snake." Paul's not condoning that kind of rationalization.

Also, notice that Paul, a champion for the health of the soul, isn't afraid to tell Timothy to take care of his body. Medicine is not the enemy of faith. God has given us skilled doctors, pharmacists, nurses, and surgeons to treat the body. Sure, medicine can be abused. But that's no reason to stay away from those who are skilled in treating the body.

Incidentally, exercise isn't faith's enemy either. "The more spiritual you get, the more you should neglect your body" is faulty thinking. Scripture nowhere tells us to neglect or abuse our bodies. We need to take care of them.

We need to balance the physical with the spiritual. Today, Paul might say, "No longer read books exclusively, but get out and exercise" or "No longer be serious and intense exclusively, but laugh, have fun, broaden yourself."

Prognosis: Hope

Paul's instruction provides us with an inoculation: hope.

First, there's *unseen and intangible hope* because God, Christ, and the angels observe and care about our ministry (1 Tim. 5:21). Talk about accountability!

Second, there's *tangible and earthly hope*. When the right people are ordained for leadership or welcomed back into the body after a bout with sin (v. 22), we can see the eternal at work on earth.

Third, there's *physical hope* because God cares about our bodies as well as our souls. He's interested in the well-being of our whole person (v. 23).

Fourth, there's *relational hope* because God is at work, even when we cannot do the job. He succeeds even when we fail. He exposes and judges sin according to His own timing and glory (vv. 24–25). And He supervises the selection of leaders.

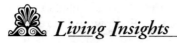 *Living Insights*

The murmurs travel through the community like the voices of onlookers analyzing a crash scene. "The pastor had too much power, too much control," one voice says. "That's why the church split. He should have allowed the congregation to have more input."

"No," says another. "The congregation's to blame. They should have trusted and submitted to their leaders. They're just a bunch of crybabies who had to have everything their own way. The sheep tried to lead the church instead of letting the shepherds do it."

Whatever the sordid details, church government and structure aside, one thing is a sure bet: sin wasn't dealt with when it should have been. Most likely, it was allowed to fester until the church grew sick beyond hope of rehabilitation. The pastor's resistance to counsel and his controlling nature were overlooked by people who believed a leader is somehow exempt from accountability. On the other hand, some members of the congregation disguised their gossip, nit-picking, and personal attacks on the pastor as prayer requests, righteous wrath, or concern for the rest of the flock.

Sin is sin, regardless of who commits it or what we choose to call it. Living in the grace of Christ doesn't give us license to ignore or disguise sin. God expects His people to reflect Him not only in their belief but in their behavior.

Would you say that your church takes sin seriously?

_____

_____

Are such truths as God's holiness, His perfect standard, and the reality of our fallen nature taught along with other truths such as His grace, love, forgiveness, and tender care for us? In other words, are all the facets of the jewel of God's nature held before the light for the congregation to see?

_____

_____

Does your church leadership believe in applying church discipline if necessary? Under what conditions would they apply it?

_____

_____

_____

_____

Is your pastor accountable? To whom? How does he respond to legitimate confrontation?

_____

_____

_____

Would you say that your church has been honest and impartial in dealing with sin? Have you?

_____

_____

_____

Sin is like a stubborn weed. The longer we ignore it, the stronger and higher it grows. God has given us His Word, His Spirit, His Son, and one another to help with the landscaping. But first, we have to admit that we have weeds.

Chapter 16

RESPONDING CORRECTLY TO AUTHORITY

1 Timothy 6:1–6

Had you lived in the Roman-dominated world of the first century, you would have understood authority in a much different way than we do today. There's a good chance you would have been one of sixty million slaves—half the population of the empire. This thread of slavery was woven tightly into the fabric of Roman culture. One hard tug and the whole garment would have unraveled.

Slavery, to be sure, was an effective system—how else would Rome have achieved such durable economic, political, and military might? Nevertheless, it was a corrupt system, because it regarded human beings as mere property to be used, and abused, at an owner's discretion.

How would you, a slave who had found freedom in Christ, have responded to your situation? Would you have tried to dismantle such an oppressive institution by organizing a revolt? "Stop serving your masters," you might have instructed. "Don't submit. Strike back!" You might even have encouraged fellow slaves to take up arms against the empire itself.

But would that have been the most effective—or the most Christlike—response? The Roman army, after all, was equipped to snuff out the first flicker of rebellion.

This was the world Paul lived in. And he knew what course of action would most impact the Roman world *and* bring glory to God. Not rebellion . . . but submission.

Let's Admit It

That plan still applies today. Though we no longer have slavery, we all have to deal with authority. Each of us, regardless of our occupation or place in life, is under someone's, and ultimately God's, authority.

Before we can learn to respond properly to authority, however, we need to admit that this isn't a "quick fix" issue. Developing a biblical perspective on this subject, like everything else in life, requires some effort. So let's start by taking a realistic look at four facts about authority.

1. *Submitting to authority is not a natural trait.* As a sinful people,

we prefer rebellion over submission. Rebellion's more fun, more adventurous, more self-gratifying. Being our own boss, we think, allows us to keep tighter control over our life. This is especially true in America, a country born out of revolution, and one that is built on independent thinking and living.

2. *Struggles with authority are sometimes complex and not easily solved.* Some of us struggle with authority because we were stifled in our personal growth and expression by its misuse, or worse, we were wounded and scarred by its abuse. The hurt and confusion may be deep-seated, so it's not realistic to think that one or two Scripture verses will instantly resolve all our problems. Rather, we must recognize that understanding, growth, and change are a process. And this study might be only one link in the chain of healing God wants to take us through.

3. *Some in authority have not earned our respect.* It's hard to work for someone you don't respect. But sometimes we find ourselves in a situation that demands we do just that. A private in the army, for example, may serve under a captain who has no integrity. But if that private is wise, he'll still salute the uniform when it walks by. In the corporate world, a good human resources department will often help smooth out employee/boss disputes. Sometimes, however, we have to hang in there and try to learn what God has to teach us.

4. *Resisting authority is not always wrong.* Submitting to authority doesn't mean dispensing with discernment. Christians should be wary of anyone who demands a "follow me no matter what" kind of commitment. If denying God's moral standards or staining the good name of Christ is required, then authority should be resisted. In those cases, we need to say with the apostle Peter, "We must obey God rather than men" (Acts 5:29; see also Exod. 1:15–21).

Let's Hear It

This chapter, however, deals with *submission* to authority. So let's hear what 1 Timothy 6:1–6 has to say.

When Non-Christians Are in Authority over Us

> Let all who are under the yoke as slaves regard their own masters as worthy of all honor so that the name of God and our doctrine may not be spoken against. (v. 1)

The comparison of a slave to a yoked beast is an appropriate one, as commentators Barton, Veerman, and Wilson explain.

> Slaves conducted most of the functions of society, from the most menial tasks to work as tutors for children and estate managers. They were used as we use tools, machinery, and technology today. Slavery was economic rather than racially motivated. People usually became slaves as a result of war or poverty.
>
> A great social and legal gulf separated masters and slaves. Paul's word choice, *under the yoke*, captures the essence of slavery—most slaves were treated no better than cattle, than mere property.[1]

Christian slaves, in this often harsh and unfair environment, were still to *honor* their masters. That's the same word used in 5:3 ("honor widows") and 5:17 ("double honor"). Paul didn't mean that slaves had to buy into everything their non-believing masters believed or practiced. Rather, slaves were to treat them with respect. Work hard for them. Be honest. And not despise them because they were non-Christians.

Why would Paul want a Christian not only to remain in such bondage but also to honor the master? He says nothing here about rebelling against the system or trying to change the master. Rather, he suggests that a slave's attitude and quality of his or her work will preserve a good reputation for Christianity.

Also, the Romans, who regarded Caesar as their chief god, feared the new King to whom the growing number of Christians paid homage. Stamping out these "traitors" was at the root of their desperate persecutions. The kingdom of Christ, though, is more than just another political opponent or threatening power base that takes control by force. To get the Roman world to understand this, Paul saw that influence, not insubordination, was the only way to change the empire.

Now let's apply this to today's business environment. Christians are scattered throughout the marketplace, many under the authority of non-Christian employers. Some of those employers are people of integrity; others are bad-tempered or partial to their favorites. Some may even go out of their way to give their Christian employees a

1. Bruce B. Barton, David R. Veerman, and Neil Wilson, *1 Timothy, 2 Timothy, Titus*, Life Application Bible Commentary series (Wheaton, Ill.: Tyndale House Publishers, 1993), p. 114.

hard time—handing them the most unpleasant tasks or mocking their faith. Regardless of their attitude, Paul would tell us to honor them by doing our best on the job. Obviously, if a boss required us to do something sinful, we should resist. But we can honor non-Christian bosses without subscribing to their beliefs or lifestyle.

The workplace should not be a venue for confrontive evangelism or a forum for political activism. Yes, we're to talk about our faith at appropriate times and take a stand on moral issues. But we were hired to do a job; let's be sure that fact doesn't escape us. According to Paul's instruction, our attitude and work habits speak volumes about our faith. In fact, when others notice our commitment and hard work, we'll likely have more opportunities to share the gospel than we would if we sloughed off.

When Christians Are in Authority over Us

What if the boss is a Christian? Again, Paul's words to slaves apply to today's marketplace.

> And let those who have believers as their masters not be disrespectful to them because they are brethren, but let them serve them all the more, because those who partake of the benefit are believers and beloved. Teach and preach these principles. (v. 2)

If the boss knows Christ, we don't have to worry about the quality of our work, right? We can sort of slack off. "Hey, I'm a brother in the Lord; give me a break. Look, we're equal before God. No reason for you to get carried away with this boss thing." Guess again. Since our Christian superiors are fellow believers, we should "serve them *all the more*."

Whether we get our paycheck from a Christian organization or a secular one, we should work for our Christian bosses with special care and attention. Why? Because we're members of the same family, the beloved of Christ.

Christian bosses should take note too. Don't take advantage of your Christian employees just because you believe their faith will let you get away with it. Remember, your relationship with them goes beyond the workplace. You're part of the same family. Having authority does not grant anyone the right to mistreat others (see Eph. 6:9; Col. 4:1).

When God's Word Is in Authority over Us

When Paul exhorts Timothy to "teach and preach these things" (v. 2b), he reminds us that we're under the authority of God's Word. Some, however, resist that authority, even rebel against it.

> If anyone advocates a different doctrine, and does not agree with sound words, those of our Lord Jesus Christ, and with the doctrine conforming to godliness, he is conceited and understands nothing; but he has a morbid interest in controversial questions and disputes about words, out of which arise envy, strife, abusive language, evil suspicions, and constant friction between men of depraved mind and deprived of the truth, who suppose that godliness is a means of gain. (1 Tim. 6:3–5)

It's as though Paul is saying, "While we're on the topic of authority, let's talk about the authority of God's Word." It's no surprise that Paul comes back to this topic, since several passages in this letter exhort Timothy to confront false doctrine with the truth of holy Scripture.

Teachers in Ephesus who had no regard for the Word of God were advancing a "different doctrine" (v. 3a). *Different* in Greek is the same word translated *strange* in 1:3, which clearly refers to teaching opposite that of the gospel.

Paul isn't talking about a member of the congregation who has a slightly different interpretation from the pastor's on a minor issue—such as how many elders the church should have, the exact timing of the Second Coming, and so on. No, Paul is warning Timothy about the person who is trying to poison the teaching of God's Word with false doctrine. His teaching is unhealthy; it contradicts the words of the Lord Jesus Himself. Such teaching clouds the gospel, discourages godly behavior, and elevates human works.

Who would propagate such falsehood? Verses 4 and 5 tell us that they are people who have an inflated opinion of themselves. Their thinking is haywire. And they love to create division in the body. Now, if you think we're being hard on false teachers, look at how J. B. Phillips describes them:

> He is a conceited idiot! His mind is a morbid jumble of disputation and argument, things which lead to nothing but jealousy, quarreling, insults and malicious

126

innuendoes—continual wrangling, in fact, among men of warped minds who have lost their real hold on the truth but hope to make some profit out of the Christian religion. (vv. 4–5)

Ever known anyone like that? This isn't someone who wants to engage in a discussion of truth for the purpose of deeper learning and godly living. This person advances untruth in order to cause division. Greed for financial gain may even be the goal (v. 5b). Whatever the intent, we can be certain it's not a fuller understanding of the truth or the advancement of the gospel.

Lest Timothy misinterpret Paul to mean that godliness has no reward, he adds:

But godliness actually is a means of great gain, when accompanied by contentment. (v. 6)

When contentment is present in our spiritual lives, godliness is its own reward, as commentators Barton, Veerman, and Wilson explain.

Godliness does not come and go with the uncertainties of material wealth; godliness, with contentment, is the wealth, independent of one's bankbook and possessions. The false teachers had it backward.[2]

Contentment, as Philip H. Towner observes,

had a prominent place in Stoic philosophy, where it defined an attitude of "self-sufficiency," meaning detachment or independence from things or possessions. Contentment came from within. Paul approved of this idea but naturally supplied a Christian basis for it: "I have learned to be content whatever the circumstances. . . . I can do everything through him who gives me strength" (Phil. 4:11, 13). Thus for Paul the Christian goal is genuine relationship with God, our source of contentment, and a healthy detachment from material things.[3]

2. Barton, Veerman, and Wilson, *1 Timothy, 2 Timothy, Titus*, p. 122.

3. Philip H. Towner, *1–2 Timothy and Titus*, The IVP New Testament Commentary Series (Downers Grove, Ill.: InterVarsity Press, 1994), pp. 137–38.

God's Word reveals Christ as our only source of real contentment. Keeping ourselves under the authority of God and His Word helps us resist the temptation to find our fulfillment outside of Christ.

Let's Do It

OK, let's put this advice on authority into action. Here are some closing thoughts that will help.

1. *With the non-Christian superior, let's leave that person no room to question our faith.* This doesn't mean we have to agree with everything our superiors do; there will surely be some disagreement. But let's live and work in a way that honors Christ. Do our assignments well. Respect everyone with whom we work. And keep our spiritual fire stoked, so it will continue to burn even in the coldest work environment.

2. *With the Christian superior or subordinate, let's refuse to take unfair advantage.* Be a good employee. Work hard. View your superiors as brothers or sisters in Christ. Take special care to serve them well. And be a good boss. Be fair, ethical, supportive of the people under you. Model the behavior you expect from them. And remember, regardless of job distinctions, your subordinates stand as your equals before Christ.

3. *With Scripture, let's go beyond mere discussion to application.* This isn't a call to avoid the thoughtful reflection and discussion of Scripture. As R. C. Sproul says, "We are what we think. When our thoughts are corrupted, our lives follow suit."[4] But we can spend hours analyzing 1 Corinthians 13—yes, even in the original Greek—and still not love one another. If we truly submit to God's Word, it will show up in the way we live.

 Living Insights

No sphere of life is without authority. The office, the church, the home, even the community in which you live are structured for the exercise of authority. Take a moment to think about those over you. Then, using the questions below, evaluate your attitude toward them.

---

4. R. C. Sproul, *Essential Truths of the Christian Faith* (Wheaton Ill.: Tyndale House Publishers, 1992), p. vii.

In what sphere of life do you have the most difficulty with someone in authority over you? Consider work, church, home, school, civil authorities, and so on.

_____

_____

Why do you think there's a problem? Do you have a negative view of authority in general? What do you think causes that? Or is your superior simply unworthy of respect? Is he or she abusive? Unfair? Heavy-handed?

_____

_____

_____

_____

Based on the principles presented in this lesson, what can you do to remedy your situation? Change your attitude or work habits? Talk to your superior—sharing your concerns, speaking the truth in love? Or is it perhaps time to alter your environment somehow—change jobs, deal with someone else, etc.?

_____

_____

_____

_____

Whatever work you do, wherever you do it, remember that you're working for Christ.

> Whatever you do, do your work heartily, as for the Lord rather than for men; knowing that from the Lord you will receive the reward of the inheritance. It is the Lord Christ whom you serve. (Col. 3:23–24)

Chapter 17

CONTENTMENT . . . AND HOW TO *MISS* IT

1 Timothy 6:6–10, 17–19

*C*ontentment is a subjective word, a lot like *love*. Whether it's desirable or undesirable, healthy or unhealthy, worth pursuing or better left alone depends on how one defines it.

Some define *contentment* as a whimsical, "not-a-care-in-the-world" state of mind. It's a place to which we all want to escape. Where pleasure and play rule the day—like the Hundred Acre Wood, where Winnie the Pooh, after polishing off a whole jar of honey, plops himself against a tree for a sticky, satisfying nap (without losing his job).

Others see contentment as something to be avoided. It's a dangerous spiritual enemy, they say. Contentment means being satisfied with mediocrity, settling for what makes us happy instead of what makes us holy.

The scriptural definition avoids these two extremes. God's Word portrays contentment as a desirable trait, a level of satisfaction every Christian should experience. Yet it functions in the realm of reality; it retains responsibility and righteousness. Properly understood, contentment graces the Christian life and fosters gratefulness, an attitude that pleases God.

Would you describe yourself as a content person? Before you answer, let's take some time to define contentment more precisely. Then we'll see how to hold on to it in a world that tries so hard to take it away.

Contentment Analyzed

To sharpen our focus on contentment, let's start with what it is *not*. It's not laziness or selfishness. And it's certainly not complacency. Scripture denounces all of these qualities (see Prov. 6:6–11; 1 Cor. 10:24; Phil. 3:8–14). Nor is it satisfaction with mediocrity. Our God, after all, is an excellent God. And whatever our ministry, it should reflect His excellence (see 2 Pet. 1:2–11). So what is contentment?

The Meaning of Contentment

The Greek root of *content, arkeō,* suggests the idea of sufficiency, that something is enough. Paul's use of the term in 1 Timothy and other epistles, according to commentator Duane Litfin, expresses "that inner God-given sufficiency which does not depend on material circumstances."[1]

John the Baptizer used the same root word when he urged his listeners to be content with their wages (Luke 3:14). Jesus implied the importance of contentment when he warned, "Guard against every form of greed" (Luke 12:15). The writer of Hebrews also contrasted greed with contentment (Heb. 13:5–6).

Contentment, then, has to do with recognizing the sufficiency of what we have. And that recognition carries with it many benefits.

The Benefits of Contentment

First, *contentment allows current enjoyment rather than constant striving.* Content Christians don't have to wait until their salary reaches six figures to be happy. Their quality of life doesn't depend on the "Someday I'lls": "Someday, I'll have a new house; then I'll be happy. Someday, I'll be married (or single again); then I'll enjoy life. Someday, I'll join the perfect church; then I'll start to grow." Because contentment flows from the heart, it allows us to enjoy the here and now. Real contentment doesn't feed on circumstances or wishful thinking.

Second, *contentment gives us freedom to recognize and applaud another's achievements without being eaten up with envy.* Contentment releases us from unhealthy competition and comparison. The more content we are with our own lives, the more we can celebrate another's success instead of falling prey to jealousy.

Third, *contentment enables us to develop a genuinely grateful spirit.* Those who lack contentment don't know what it means to be truly thankful. By focusing on what they don't have, they lose sight of all the blessings—spiritual and material—that God has provided. And thankless people make poor Christians. Gratitude is the cornerstone of an effective witness for Christ (see 1 Thess. 5:18; Heb. 13:15).

---

1. A. Duane Litfin, "1 Timothy" in *The Bible Knowledge Commentary,* New Testament edition, ed. John F. Walvoord and Roy B. Zuck (Wheaton, Ill.: Scripture Press Publications, Victor Books, 1983), p. 746. See also 2 Corinthians 9:8 and Philippians 4:11 for other uses of the same word.

Contentment Amplified

It's no surprise that Paul addressed this topic with Timothy. With all that the young pastor had to face in Ephesus, contentment might have seemed elusive to him at times. False teachers assaulted his message. Some people discounted him because of his youth. And the needs of widows were outpacing the ability to meet them. No wonder his stomach was giving him problems.

Every ministry has its contentment-killers. Unhappy parishioners who have the gift of grumbling. The constant reality of sin. High stress, low pay, and even lower appreciation. So starting in 1 Timothy 6:6, Paul assures Timothy (and us) that the rigors of ministry—no matter how demanding—need not snuff out the flame of contentment.

Paul presents the importance of contentment by showing how it intertwines with four areas of life: godliness (1 Tim. 6:6), possessions (vv. 7–8), riches (vv. 9–10, 17), and character (vv. 18–19).

Contentment and Godliness

In the preceding verses, Paul has been describing false teachers who, among other unsavory characteristics, consider spiritual endeavors a mere path to prosperity (v. 5). Warning Timothy to avoid such thinking, Paul encourages his friend that godliness has a very real reward of its own—especially if it's enhanced by contentment.

> But godliness actually is a means of great gain, when accompanied by contentment. (v. 6)

Why wouldn't godliness be a means of great gain by itself? We *do* profit from a godly life in and of itself because we're living by God's design. However, contentment prevents things like worry and materialism from hindering our spiritual walk (compare Ps. 37; Matt. 6:24–34; 13:22).

So, simply put, godliness plus contentment equals great gain. And that gain is not mere material wealth destroyed by moth and rust and stolen by thieves (Matt. 6:19). It is the imperishable treasure of heaven, that inner peace and satisfaction of being right with God, of obeying and loving Him, of walking in the path of life (see Matt. 6:20–21; Prov. 3:13–26; Ps. 16:11).

Contentment and Possessions

If our contentment lies in wealth, however, or any other earthly possession, we're in for a big disappointment.

> For we have brought nothing into the world, so we cannot take anything out of it either. And if we have food and covering, with these we shall be content. (1 Tim. 6:7–8)

We enter this world carrying nothing, wearing nothing, owning nothing. We leave the same way. Souls can't tote luggage. A clinging attachment to earthly goods will only bring discontentment. Until we can say with Job, "Naked I came from my mother's womb, /And naked I shall return there" (Job 1:21a), we won't know contentment.

Yet we all need certain possessions for survival on this earth. We need food, water, clothing, and shelter (1 Tim. 6:8). These are necessities. That doesn't mean it's wrong to own a car, a stereo, or jewelry. But our contentment shouldn't lie in the acquisition of such things. The "he who dies with the most toys wins" attitude promotes an empty life because it never satisfies. It starts with the "need" to have a bigger, more expensive car. Then a boat. Then a summer home or two. Then . . . satisfaction eludes us. There's always someone who has more than we do. Let's distinguish between our wants and needs and not base our contentment on possessions but on Christ.

Contentment and Riches

Contrasted with those who are content with the basics are those who want to amass wealth.

> But those who want to get rich fall into temptation and a snare and many foolish and harmful desires which plunge men into ruin and destruction. For the love of money is a root of all sorts of evil, and some by longing for it have wandered away from the faith, and pierced themselves with many a pang. (vv. 9–10)

"Those who want to get rich" exhibit more than just a passing fancy to have more money. Commentator Donald Guthrie writes:

> The words apply to all whose aims are controlled by the passion to increase material possessions, yet there is here no condemnation of such possessions in themselves.[2]

2. Donald Guthrie, *The Pastoral Epistles*, 2d ed. (Grand Rapids, Mich.: William B. Eerdmans Publishing Co., 1990), p. 125.

These people are driven by the lure of money. Their guiding light is the glitter of silver and gold, which lures them to their destruction (see also Prov. 20:21; 28:20, 22). Philip H. Towner vividly describes the downward spiral taken by those who lust for riches.

> First, the pursuit of wealth leads down a road filled with every variety of pitfall. The words *temptation* and *trap* may well be used with Satan's manipulations in mind (3:7), and the Enemy is certainly capable of using the hope of wealth to blur the moral distinctions of believers. *Foolish and harmful desires* not only are for wealth itself but are probably also immoral cravings unleashed by access to wealth. Wealth leads people into circles where the rules are different, the peer pressure is tremendous, and the values are totally distorted. What, for the believer, might have been unthinkable from the outside becomes quite natural once on the inside. And the end of this is utter devastation, which Paul emphasizes with a verb that means to *plunge* (as if to drown) and two nouns that combine to describe complete *destruction*. Let the reader beware, for there are no such warning signs along the path to riches.[3]

The lure of money is even strong enough to entice some away from the faith, leaving the debris of broken promises and relationships in its wake (1 Tim. 6:10).

Notice, though, that money itself is not the problem; our attitude toward it is. Money is amoral, neither good nor bad. But the "love of money" is the root of all kinds of evil and leads to destruction. Put another way, it's not what we have that causes problems, it's what has us.

What about those who are already rich? How are they to view their wealth?

> Instruct those who are rich in this present world not to be conceited or to fix their hope on the uncertainty of riches, but on God, who richly supplies us with all things to enjoy. (v. 17)

3. Philip H. Towner, *1–2 Timothy and Titus*, The IVP New Testament Commentary Series (Downers Grove, Ill.: InterVarsity Press, 1994), p. 139.

First, the rich are to avoid being conceited, looking down on those who have less (see also Prov. 14:21; 17:5; 22:2). Second, they're not to fix their hope on a false security (see also Prov. 23:4–5). And third, we are all to see our possessions as belonging to God and given by Him for His glory and our enjoyment (see also 1 Cor. 3:21b–23).

Contentment and Character

Those who have been blessed materially by God have a great opportunity to display His character in how they handle money.

> Instruct them to do good, to be rich in good works, to be generous and ready to share, storing up for themselves the treasure of a good foundation for the future, so that they may take hold of that which is life indeed. (vv. 18–19)

Paul would give these instructions to the rich. "Help others" would be his first piece of counsel. Don't let your wealth insulate you from the real needs of others. Rather, take the genuine role of a servant and find ways to benefit other people with your money. "Get involved" would be the next instruction—let your involvement match the size of your income. By giving generously, we not only help those in need; we store up riches for ourselves in heaven.

Contentment Applied

Contentment isn't a formula. There's no pill we can swallow to instantly achieve it. Instead, it is a by-product of a close walk with God. Nevertheless, here are some closing thoughts to keep us from missing out on contentment as we grow in Christ.

First, *we'll miss contentment if something other than food, clothing, or shelter becomes essential.* We must have the basics to survive. But for many of us, the "basics" include more wants than needs, more luxuries than necessities. The fewer amenities we need to make us happy, the more content we'll be.

Second, *we'll miss contentment if having more money than we currently make becomes a fixation.* Don't misunderstand. Raises are good. Promotions are too. There's nothing wrong with a salary that's commensurate with skill and experience. And there's nothing wrong with making sound investments to increase financial stability. But does your contentment depend on more and bigger dollar signs?

Third, *we will miss contentment if keeping rather than releasing becomes our objective.* What's your first thought when a windfall blows your way? "What can I get?" or "What can I give?" There's more contentment in helping than in hoarding. No wonder Jesus said, "It is more blessed to give than to receive" (Acts 20:35). And He should know.

We are most content when we're grateful for what we own, satisfied with what we make, and generous to those in need.

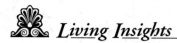 ## Living Insights

Paul wasn't asking Timothy do to anything he hadn't done himself. He told the Philippians,

> But I rejoiced in the Lord greatly, that now at last you have revived your concern for me; indeed, you were concerned before, but you lacked opportunity. Not that I speak from want; for I have learned to be content in whatever circumstances I am. I know how to get along with humble means, and I also know how to live in prosperity; in any and every circumstance I have learned the secret of being filled and going hungry, both of having abundance and suffering need. I can do all things through Him who strengthens me. (Phil. 4:10–13)

When Paul wrote to the Philippians, he faced a predicament. On the one hand, he was compelled to thank that church for their generous gift. On the other hand, he didn't want them to think that he had been sitting around waiting for the money to come in or that his joy or fulfillment in ministry depended on their giving. So he sent them his heartfelt thanks, but he also reminded them that his source of strength, and contentment, was Christ Himself.

Can you say that? Would Christ be as real, as dear, as worthy of your devotion if most of your possessions suddenly vanished? Or does your contentment climb, dip, and dive like a kite in the circumstantial breezes?

_____

_____

_____

Is there anything (or anyone) you're clutching too tightly? Something (or someone) that might be keeping you from knowing Christ more intimately?

_____

_____

_____

Are there any changes you need to consider making?

_____

_____

_____

Contentment isn't found in a place; it's in a Person. It doesn't come by escaping reality but by embracing a relationship. If contentment seems like a distant glimmer on the horizon to you, maybe it's time to refresh yourself with the truth of Christ's nearness, sufficiency, and abundant provision. Meditating on the following passages can help you do just that.

Psalm 23 _____

_____

_____

Luke 12:16–32 _____

_____

_____

Ephesians 1:18–23 _____

_____

_____

Chapter 18

CLEAR COMMANDMENTS
OF GODLINESS
1 Timothy 6:11–16

White-water rafting. Northwest Colorado, somewhere near the Wyoming border.

You've had an exhilarating but safe day. A few moderate rapids, not much more than speed bumps in the water. But sufficient to learn on. Time to rest now and enjoy nighttime by the river. The pip-pop of a blazing campfire. A black velvet heaven sprayed with stars so clear and bright you can almost count them. And tomorrow? Cujo. The meanest, hungriest rapids on the river. Get some sleep; you'll need all your wits in the morning.

You hear the rapids long before you see them. "Listen," says the guide, holding up one hand. "Just around the next turn." The paddles are still as each person in the raft stops to soak in the sound of rushing water . . . and adjust their life vests. Louder and louder the sound roars, like wet thunder, until it finally drowns out the thump-thump of your racing heart.

Around the bend . . . and there they are. Foaming and froth-ing like a rabid beast. A beast that loses all reason, all sanity, at the sight of a gray rubber vessel. And the only way down the river is straight through its jaws.

At this point, following orders can save your life. When the guide yells, "Hard right!" you don't stop to discuss the finer points of maneuvering; that was done on the bank. You must respond with instant speed and strength. The choice is simple: obey the command . . . or be Cujo's next meal.

Navigating the spiritual life is a lot like shooting the rapids. There's a time for discussion and for pondering spiritual truth. And there's a time to jump into action—just because God said to do it.

Paul, knowing he's nearing the end of his letter, begins to sum up his instructions to Timothy with a firm "Just do it!" First Timothy 6:11–16 is loaded with imperative verbs and brimming with black-and-white commands. It's as though Paul is saying, "If you don't want to be eaten alive in ministry, Timothy, then do these things. Don't dally. Obey. And you'll not only survive, you'll honor God."

Following orders can save your life—on the river and in the spiritual life.

Some Things to Remember about Commandments

Before plunging into Paul's specific commands to Timothy, let's get our feet wet with a look at commandments in general.

All of God's Word is instructive (2 Tim. 3:16). But it instructs in a variety of ways. God has revealed His character and His will in many kinds of literature—historical narrative, poetry, parables, epistles, and so on. Another way to look at God's instruction is to divide it into precepts and principles.

Precepts are direct moral commands. Black-and-white. Clear boundaries. They don't require a lot of painstaking interpretation or sifting through cultural grids. The Ten Commandments, for example, are precepts (see Exod. 20:3–17). And so is Jesus' Great Commission in Matthew 28:19.

Principles, however, aren't always direct or clear at first glance. They are no less instructive or important, but they require more pondering, more digging than precepts do. Principles are broader. They address the "gray areas" of life about which the Scriptures don't lay out clear commands. Principles help us answer such questions as "Is it OK for me to go to the movies?" "How much should I be 'in the world' in order to evangelize the lost?" and "When is it right to resist the civil authorities?"

"Don't abuse your freedom in Christ" is a biblical principle derived from 1 Corinthians 8 and Romans 14:13–23. But what does that mean? When do I step over the line of enjoying my freedom and begin abusing it? And is that line located in different places for different people?

Here's another way to think about precepts or commandments. They usually exhibit the following four characteristics:

1. They are brief, simple, and clear.

2. They are for our good and God's glory.

3. They call for one response: obedience.

4. If we disobey them, there are serious consequences.

Some Commandments to Obey regarding Ministry

First Timothy 6:11–16 is swirling with precepts. Just look at the imperatives: "Flee" (v. 11), "pursue" (v. 11), "fight" (v. 12), "take hold" (v. 12), "keep" (v. 14). Not a lot of room for speculation here. Like the "Hard right!" of the river guide, such commands have our good in mind and call for immediate and consistent obedience. Let's look at each one of these commands and see how our obedience to them can keep our own ministry on course.

Flee Godlessness

Sometimes the bravest thing to do in the Christian life, and in leadership in particular, is run away. Some rapids shouldn't be attempted, regardless of our skill, experience, or determination. So Paul isn't elevating cowardice when he says to Timothy,

> But flee from these things, you man of God. (v. 11a)

"These things" are the attitudes and practices that characterize the false teachers—anti-gospel rhetoric, pride, preoccupation with trivial disputes, divisiveness, greed, and so on (vv. 3–10). As a "man of God," Timothy's life should display traits opposite those of the false teachers. So Paul advises him to "flee" such things. The present imperative verb indicates a continuing action. In other words, "Keep on fleeing these things; make it a habit, a lifestyle."

But running from wrong is only half the plan for godliness. We must also run *toward* what is right.

Pursue Godliness

> Pursue righteousness, godliness, faith, love, perseverance and gentleness. (v. 11b)

Paul is so straightforward here that we only need to look briefly at each of these priceless virtues to get a handle on them.

- *Righteousness* is a state of heart and mind that operates in harmony with the living God.

- *Godliness* is an authentic and abiding desire to glorify God.

- *Faith* means that rather than living by sight, rather than framing all of our opinions on the basis of the seen and the tangible, we will trust God to open doors. We'll wait on Him to clear the pathways and solve the conflicts.

- *Love* seeks the highest good of the other person.

- *Perseverance* means "to abide under." It carries the idea of handling our lives in a stable, enduring, fluid manner.

- *Gentleness* is strength under control, composure—especially in the face of opposition and wrong.[1]

Philip H. Towner draws all these virtues together to help us see the big picture.

> The six virtues together describe the lifestyle of balanced spirituality that ought to characterize the Christian. A Christian leader must be a model of these things. A holistic portrait, it encompasses one's walk with God and disposition toward unbelievers. Are these standards impossibly high? If we think in terms of human effort, yes; but with the high calling to ministry also go vast resources for godly living.[2]

How about you? Are you content merely to flee godlessness? Or are you in constant pursuit of godliness? We've said it in previous chapters, but it's worth repeating: The Christlike life doesn't just happen. It's deliberate. It requires focus, discipline, and a dependence on the One who Himself possesses all those traits.

Fight the Good Fight

One would hardly expect Paul to exhort us to fight after just having encouraged us to be gentle. But he does.

> Fight the good fight of faith. (v. 12a)

Contradictory? No. Paul isn't describing an attitude of pugnaciousness but a struggling against all odds to keep one's faith strong and growing. The Greek carries the idea of contending for a prize in the Olympic games. Athletic competition requires discipline, training, and movement toward a specified goal (see also 2 Tim. 2:1–7). For Timothy, and all Christians, that goal is eternal life.

Take Hold of Eternal Life

> Take hold of the eternal life to which you were

---

1. Gerhard Kittel and Gerhard Friedrich, eds., *Theological Dictionary of the New Testament*, translated and abridged by Geoffrey W. Bromiley (1985; reprint, Grand Rapids, Mich.: William B. Eerdmans Publishing Co., 1992), p. 803.

2. Philip H. Towner, *1–2 Timothy and Titus*, The IVP New Testament Commentary Series (Downers Grove, Ill.: InterVarsity Press, 1994), pp. 141–42.

called, and you made the good confession in the presence of many witnesses. (1 Tim. 6:12b)

Eternal life is our motivation to stay in the fight, to keep contending for the faith, to keep our raft on course—no matter how rough the waters. By urging Timothy to "take hold" of eternal life, Paul isn't suggesting that he save himself; salvation is by grace alone. And Timothy has already been "called" into eternal life. Rather, Paul wants Timothy to remember his goal, to get a grip on eternal kind of living. "Hold fast to it. Don't let it slip through your fingers. Don't go back to the old ways."

The "good confession in the presence of many witnesses" probably refers to Timothy's baptism, where he made a public profession of his faith in Christ. Paul's reminder of this event reinforces the command to take hold of eternal life. For when would the truth of Christ, the joy of His grace, the sense of freedom, the wonder of His love been more heightened for Timothy than at his baptism? It's as though Paul is saying, "Remember how real eternal life was to you that day. It's still that real. So live it just like you did when you first confessed it."

Keep the Commandment

Paul now gives perhaps his strongest exhortation to Timothy in the whole letter.

> I charge you in the presence of God, who gives life to all things, and of Christ Jesus, who testified the good confession before Pontius Pilate, that you keep the commandment without stain or reproach until the appearing of our Lord Jesus Christ, which He will bring about at the proper time. (vv. 13–15a)

Just as Jesus stayed blamelessly true to His calling before Pilate, so Timothy is to stay true to "the commandment" and give his accusers no reason to find blame in him. This "commandment"

> is probably broader than any single law. It refers to the entire body of sound teaching Paul had been describing throughout the letter. Timothy, by his own godly life and by his faithful ministry, was to preserve this body of truth from stain or reproach until the appearing (cf. 2 Tim. 1:10; 4:1, 8; Titus 2:13) of our Lord Jesus Christ. Then and only then will

the struggle (1 Tim. 6:12) be over.[3]

This section closes, as it should, with praise to our source for godly living, our strength for excellent ministry—the Lord God Himself.

> He who is the blessed and only Sovereign, the King of kings and Lord of lords; who alone possesses immortality and dwells in unapproachable light; whom no man has seen or can see. To Him be honor and eternal dominion! Amen. (vv. 15b–16)

Some Attitudes to Maintain While Obeying

Remember, obedience to the King of kings was never meant to resemble that of an oppressed commoner to a cruel despot. Obedience, for the Christian, should flow from a heart that loves and wants to please the God who has gone to great lengths to love us first (see 1 John 4:19). It's not mechanical compliance. It's living, loving acquiescence that pulses with the attitudes of unswerving devotion (1 Tim. 6:11), disciplined determination (v. 12), absolute purity (vv. 13–14), and true humility (vv. 15–16).

Sure, the spiritual waters can get rough. But we have a Guide who knows the river by heart and will never steer us wrong.

 Living Insights

Sometimes we get overwhelmed when we see a string of commands like the one running through 1 Timothy 6:11–16. Why? Because we think that we, in our own strength, have to muster the ability to keep them. But that isn't God's plan. It never has been.

God gave us His law and has required us to keep it, yet He knew that we would never be able to satisfy His demands for holiness in our own strength. Because we are sinful people, we rebel against God's law; we're not able to please Him and satisfy His requirements (compare Rom. 7:7–8). Hence our need for Christ, the only One who ever kept the law perfectly.

---

3. A. Duane Litfin, "1 Timothy," in *The Bible Knowledge Commentary*, New Testament edition, ed. John F. Walvoord and Roy B. Zuck (Wheaton, Ill.: Scripture Press Publications, Victor Books, 1983), p. 747.

Our union with Christ enables us to please God. Our hopelessness to keep the law is what drives us to the holiness of Christ. "Before God can give us the gospel," says James Montgomery Boice, "he must slay us with the law."[4] For those of us who know Christ, the despair created by failing God's standards is only temporary. Failure for the Christian doesn't lead to judgment but to the grace of Christ, which renders us acceptable to God. Boice continues,

> [Being raised with Christ] means that all who believe in Christ are united to him so that his life becomes available to them. We may be weak and utterly helpless, unable to resist temptation for a single minute. But he is strong, and he lives to give help and deliverance at every moment. Victory, therefore, is no longer a question of our strength but of his power. His power is what we need.[5]

So take God's commands seriously, and work to please Him. But when you fail, remember that God doesn't abandon us, because He has clothed us in the righteousness of His Son, who died for our sins and kept the law without fail (1 Cor. 1:30–31; Gal. 3:24–27).

---

4. James Montgomery Boice, *Foundations of the Christian Faith*, revised in one volume (Downers Grove, Ill.: InterVarsity Press, 1986), p. 225.

5. Boice, *Foundations of the Christian Faith*, p. 345.

Chapter 19

A TREASURE WORTH GUARDING

1 Timothy 6:20–21

Good morning, Mr. Bailey. I guess you forgot something."
Uncle Billy couldn't imagine what the teller was talking about.

"Aren't you going to make a deposit?"

"Sure," said Uncle Billy.

"Then it's usually customary to bring the money with you."

William Bailey's look of bewilderment gave way to an enlightened smile. He had lived with his own absentmindedness for many years now, tying strings around his fingers to remember important appointments or the whereabouts of valuables. He forgot a lot, but he usually managed to take care of the essentials. The money was on his person somewhere, he was certain. After all, no one's forgetful enough to misplace eight thousand dollars in cash.

He reached into his inner coat pocket and . . . no money. The smile disappeared. Vest pockets. Empty. The line of customers behind Uncle Billy lengthened as he frisked himself in a frenzied attempt to produce the cash. He left the teller's window and began to retrace his steps.

In the bank president's office, old man Potter unfolded his morning newspaper and discovered a crinkled, unsealed envelope stuffed with cash—eight thousand dollars worth. Just a few minutes earlier, Uncle Billy had stopped Potter in the lobby and snatched his newspaper to gloat over an article about his nephew, Harry Bailey, who had been declared a war hero. Somehow the envelope got folded up in the paper just before Uncle Billy gave it back to Potter.

Potter cracked his office door and peered into the lobby, where Uncle Billy was working himself into a panic. He stopped at the counter where he had filled out the deposit slip. He clawed through the trash can below the counter and found only wads of white paper. Then he spun through the bank's revolving door, hoping to track down the fugitive envelope on the snow-crusted sidewalk.

Potter sat up straight in his wheelchair and contemplatively stroked his wicked chin. This was his chance, at last, to ruin the Bailey Building and Loan—the only establishment left in Bedford Falls keeping Potter from taking over the whole town. For years the Baileys had been like flies buzzing around Potter's web of greed and control. But they had been too decent, too honest, too smart to light. Until now.

If you've seen Frank Capra's classic film *It's a Wonderful Life*, you know it has a happy ending. George Bailey (played by Jimmy Stewart), Uncle Billy's nephew and president of the Bailey Building and Loan, averts the bankruptcy and scandal he thinks are inevitable. All the people he has treated kindly over the years scrape their pockets and show up at George's house with more than enough money to bail out his business. And old man Potter, once again, is defeated by kindness.

If someone does a sequel, though, one wonders if George could ever again trust Uncle Billy to handle the money. After all, he had been entrusted with a deposit, and he let it slip through his fingers. His carelessness endangered not only his own livelihood but that of the entire Bailey family and the employees of the Building and Loan. In fact, it nudged the whole town up to the precipice of disaster.

You and I have been entrusted with a deposit too—our scriptural, orthodox faith. We can guard it, protect it, and enrich others with it. Or we can neglect it and leave its doctrines for thieves to pilfer, plunder, and pervert for their own wicked purposes.

Knowing that the thieves of truth—false teachers—lurked around the dark corners of Ephesus, Paul closed his letter to Timothy with a final admonition: Guard the deposit. And like a brightly colored string tied around our finger, the apostle's words remind us to do the same.

A Tone of Urgency

It seems to go without saying that Christians should have a healthy respect for the essentials of their faith. That they should hold it dear, protect it. So why does Paul have to *command* Timothy to do it? Because Timothy is surrounded by false teachers who want to bankrupt our faith by circulating counterfeit doctrine. Paul's whole letter, in fact, resonates with a tone of urgency to guard the truth from spiritual thieves (see 1:3–4, 18–19; 3:14–16; 4:1–3, 6–7, 10–16; 6:11–16, 20).

Churches today would do well to exude such urgency, particularly where the integrity of Scripture is concerned. In many places God's Word is being watered down, made more palatable for the masses. The niceties of a good life have overshadowed the necessity of the Cross. The pursuit of happiness has supplanted the practice of holiness. Claiming success gets more pulpit time than confessing sin. And serious study of Scripture has fallen prey to unbridled emotionalism. People are starving for the truth. That's urgent!

Guard the Deposit

So it is with urgency that Paul says,

> O Timothy, guard what has been entrusted to you. (v. 20a)

Commentator William Barclay brings out the imagery behind Paul's words.

> The passage talks of the *trust* that has been entrusted to him. The Greek word for *trust* is *paratheke*, which literally means a *deposit*. It is the word for money deposited with a banker or with a friend. When such money was in time demanded back, it was a sacred duty to hand it back entire. Sometimes children [in Roman society] were called a *paratheke*, a sacred trust. If the gods gave a man a child, it was his duty to present that child trained and equipped to the gods. The Christian faith is like that, something which we received from our forefathers, and which we must pass on to our children. . . .
> . . . If in our day the Church were to become enfeebled; if the Christian ethic were to be more and more submerged in the world; if the Christian faith were to be twisted and distorted; it would not only be we who were the losers, those of generations still to come would be robbed of something infinitely precious. We are not only the possessors but also the trustees of the faith.[1]

And ultimately, that which we have received from God we must

---

1. William Barclay, *The Letters to Timothy, Titus, and Philemon*, rev. ed., The Daily Study Bible series (Philadelphia, Pa.: Westminster Press, 1975), p. 138.

return to Him. The life-saving truths of our faith are indeed a sacred trust.

Guard by . . . Avoiding?

> . . . avoiding worldly and empty chatter and the opposing arguments of what is falsely called "knowledge." (v. 20b)

Don't get the wrong idea from the word *avoid* (literally, *turn away*). As Philip H. Towner says, the word

> does not mean refrain from confrontation. Rather, this action represents the conscious decision not to become involved in or even contemplate the false doctrine.[2]

"Stay focused on the deposit, Timothy. Preach the Word; deliver the gospel." That's the thrust of Paul's command. The best way to expose a counterfeit is to turn on the light of truth, not immerse ourselves in or toy with untruth. We guard our faith by keeping ourselves free from the influence of false doctrine, which Paul characterizes as "empty chatter."

> Not only does it have nothing to do with God or godliness, but it is also foolish nonsense (1:6; 4:7). It may have been systematic, but in comparison with the "standard" gospel, and given the results it brought—argument, speculation, inconsistent behavior and so on—it was no more than profane nonsense.[3]

We should never be afraid to confront false doctrine or engage in debate with its proponents. But when we do, we need to keep the Word of God as our central reference point. For it is the true "knowledge" that keeps us from going astray (v. 21).

Know What's Worth Fighting For

Whenever we talk about defending the faith, we need to remember that not everything is worth fighting over or dying for. For example, Jesus Christ is the only way to God. That's worth fighting

2. Philip H. Towner, *1–2 Timothy and Titus*, The IVP New Testament Commentary Series (Downers Grove, Ill.: InterVarsity Press, 1994), p. 150.

3. Towner, *1–2 Timothy and Titus*, p. 150.

for. Salvation is by faith alone in Christ alone—we go to the wall for that one. The Word of God is infallible and authoritative. Humanity is sinful. God is holy. Jesus is God. These are all nonnegotiables. We stand atop the treasure heap, swords drawn, to preserve and defend these truths.

Some things, however, are negotiable. Like whether the doxology comes at the beginning of the worship service or the end, or whether it's even included at all. In some churches, though, you would think that tampering with the order of service is tantamount to denying the Trinity. We need to distinguish absolutes from non-absolutes. Absolutes are sourced in Scripture and never change; they remain the same from age to age, culture to culture. Non-absolutes, however, can change. They're permitted to flex with cultural trends, personal taste, and tradition—but without altering the essentials. However, when non-absolutes usurp the place of biblical principles, we have elevated them to the status of absolutes.

Here's another way to think of it: The deposit doesn't change; the way we guard it does. Consider, for example, evangelism. The message of the gospel remains the same, but our methods of spreading it may vary. We may proclaim it from the pulpit or share it with a coworker at break time. We may plan to engage an individual in a discussion of spirituality, or we may spontaneously share the gospel in response to Jehovah's Witnesses who come to our door.

The Savior we worship never changes. But we have freedom in our *style* of worship. Music may be contemporary, traditional, or a blend. We can worship God through planned liturgy or a structure that allows for more spontaneity. And there's nothing in Scripture that commands us to meet for worship three times a week.

We're even allowed some freedom in the observance of the Lord's Table. What's important is that we do it. How often should we serve it? Who exactly should serve it? Scripture doesn't specify.

And, believe it or not, there's no *ideal* size for a congregation. Preaching style, the size of the community, the age of the church, the philosophy of ministry, God's blessing—all these and more contribute to a church's size. What's important is that the body of Christ follow the Lord and stay pure, not that they break church growth records.

You see the difference between absolutes and non-absolutes? Let's keep them in perspective. And fight for the things worth fighting for.

Some Guidelines for a Guardian Mentality

As we guard the treasure of our scriptural faith, let's keep these three guidelines in mind.

1. *Our message is fixed and inflexible, not our methods.* When we put our money in the bank, we want one thing—we want it kept safe. We don't get mired in the details of the vault's construction or the names and shifts of all the bank employees. Those things change. We just want our treasure protected. The same is true with the Christian faith. We should preserve its truths but teach it, preach it, and live it with all the creativity and flexibility God allows.

2. *Our mandate is to defend the truth, not offend people.* Scripture tells us that the message of the Cross will be offensive to some, simply because they refuse to believe the truth. So let the Cross, not Christians, do the offending. Our job is to know and communicate the truth, not blow people out of the water.

3. *Our manner is to be loving, not proving.* While we're championing the truth, let's not forget to employ compassion, grace, love, and understanding. In the midst of contending for Christ, let's be Christlike.

Living Insights

Did you notice how Paul signs off? "Grace be with you" (v. 21). In a word, that's our treasure—grace. That's what the false teachers wanted to steal. And that's what they try to steal today. All false teaching is void of a true understanding of God's grace. Graceless religion leads to either life-choking legalism or unbridled libertinism.

Legalists reject the notion that God freely gives His salvation to people apart from any human works. "We must earn it," they say. So they require abstinence from movies, card games, and other activities that could be counted as a black mark in God's book. The truth is, each of us has enough black marks to fill God's book from cover to cover. We all sin; we were born with a sin nature (Rom. 3:23). Had God not reached down to us in grace, none of us would have a chance to live a life that pleases Him.

The libertines, on the other hand, define grace as freedom from any moral responsibility. Since human effort can't save us, they reason, good works have no value. We can live however we want, without consequences. But such a view fails to acknowledge that, though good works don't save us, they are the outgrowth of our salvation (Eph. 2:8–10; Phil. 2:12–13; James 2:14–26). Now that Christ lives in us, our works *are* pleasing to Him. His grace allows us to live a life of good works—something we couldn't do in our own power as non-Christians.

So remember, when we guard our faith, we're guarding God's grace, the universe's richest treasure. Without it, we would be spiritual paupers. But God's grace has made us the sons and daughters of Him who owns everything. Guard it well. And share it freely— it never runs out.

Chapter 20

LET'S EVALUATE YOUR MINISTRY

A Review of 1 Timothy

Excellence isn't automatic.

That's one thing we've learned from this study. Excellence is a hands-on quality, achieved only through the deliberate, disciplined study and application of God's Word. It requires knowing where we are and keeping an eye on where God wants us to go.

So every once in a while, we need to pull off the spiritual freeway and ask, "Is my life, my ministry, heading in the right direction?" We have to evaluate. We can't click our lives into "cruise" and assume we'll stay on course forever. We have to pull over and get our bearings.

In this final lesson of our study, let's do just that. Let's take some time out to do some evaluating. Consider this chapter one big Living Insight that will help you keep your ministry, whatever its scope and design, on the road to excellence.

Let's Think about Evaluation

In case you're wondering if evaluating your ministry is worth the time and effort, give some thought to what evaluation is and why it's important.

What Is Evaluation?

According to Webster, to *evaluate* is "to determine or fix the value of; to determine the significance, worth, or condition of usually by careful appraisal and study."[1] Here's another way to put it: to appraise, to probe, so as to discover strengths and weaknesses.

Evaluation is critical to any endeavor. A skipper evaluates the ship's course with a compass. Motorists refer to maps; pilots, to instruments. Football teams view films of the previous game to assess their performance. And corporations analyze their profit-and-loss statements to determine their health. Why should ministry be any

---

1. *Merriam-Webster's Collegiate Dictionary*, 10th ed., see "evaluate."

different? Our standard is the Word of God. By measuring ourselves against it, we can tell if we're heading straight or veering off course.

How Does Evaluation Help?

First, *evaluation brings us back to basics*. It helps us answer the questions, "What are we about?" "What are our goals?" and "Why are we doing this?" Without evaluation, we can lose sight of our purpose and mission.

Second, *evaluation helps us separate the essentials from the incidentals*. Have you ever felt as though you've got the pedal to the metal but you're not really moving—like a car fighting for traction on an icy street? That's what happens when we get lost in the incidentals. We create a lot of RPMs, but we don't get very far. There's more to ministry than busyness. Some of the things that drain our energy and attention aren't really that important; some of them, in fact, are petty. Evaluation helps us put first things first.

Third, *evaluation frees us from worry and fear*. If we'll just refocus on what's important, we'll discover that we don't have to please people or worry about things we can't control.

Fourth, *evaluation reveals our strengths and weaknesses*. Face it. There's not a church or a person on the planet who's doing it perfectly. We need to assess our ministries honestly, sharpen our strengths, and work on our weaknesses. Evaluation keeps us from resting on our laurels. It also keeps us from slipping into mediocrity.

As you can see, evaluation has benefits. But that doesn't mean it's always easy.

Why Is Evaluation So Difficult?

Evaluations are like X-rays. They can save our lives, but only by exposing trouble spots we would rather not see. That's why evaluation can be threatening—we'd much rather be encouraged than criticized. Even when we ask friends for honest feedback, and they put it in just the right way, their response can still hurt. Solomon noted this in his Proverbs:

> Faithful are the wounds of a friend,
> But deceitful are the kisses of an enemy. (27:6)

And let's face it, although exposure is the first step toward change, change is always hard. If we stop evaluating, however, we pass up the opportunity for improvement.

Let's Take a Look at Your Ministry

Taking a deep breath, then, use the main principles from each chapter of 1 Timothy as your road map to evaluate your ministry—to see where you've been and where you're going.

Chapter 1: A Ministry Must Maintain Balance

An excellent ministry is a balanced ministry. It doesn't teeter toward dangerous extremes. Notice how chapter 1 encourages us to load the scales of ministry equally.

We must balance the identification of error with the demonstration of love (vv. 3–5). Let's not sacrifice Christlike love on the altar of doctrinal purity. Sure, we need to defend the truth and expose falsehood. But we also need to *demonstrate* truth by expressing Christ's character and care. "The goal of our instruction," said Paul, "is love."

We must balance strong convictions with notable humility (vv. 11–16). No one could accuse Paul of wishy-washy Christianity; he made no apologies about his convictions. Yet he never lost sight of the One who gave him those convictions. Paul realized that everything he was, all that he stood for, flowed from the gracious and merciful hand of God.

We must balance great theology with everyday practicality. Theology starts in the head. Then it flows to the heart (v. 17) and spills into the practicalities of life. Knowledge that grows stagnant in the mind never feeds and refreshes the dryness of day-to-day living. Conversely, a Christian to-do list based on something other than prayerful study and reflection on the Word is working from a shallow reservoir. Our quality of life is directly linked to our knowledge of God.

We need to balance fighting the good fight with keeping a good conscience (vv. 18–20). Individually, like an athlete in training, we must fight passivity and stretch, sweat, and run if we're going to grow in our faith. And corporately, a ministry that fights nothing falls for anything. We must be prepared to stand against the attacks of false teachers (v. 20).

However, a ministry that does nothing but fight is a waste. People become nitpicky, negative, squint-eyed, and paranoid. They develop an exclusive, "I alone have the truth" mentality. So, in the midst of the battle, we must keep the faith with a good conscience (v. 19). That is, we must hold on to the largeness of God, the scope of our faith, and our humble need for a clean conscience.

◆

Take some time right now to assess the balance of your own life and ministry. When you discuss your faith with others, do you blend compassion and respect with your doctrinal zeal?

_____

_____

Do you know the Scriptures well enough to defend the foundational doctrines of the Christian faith yet not come across as arrogant or uncaring? In whom do you boast—yourself or Christ?

_____

_____

_____

Is Christianity for you mere head knowledge, or does the oil of the Word work its way into the moving parts of everyday life? What can you do to live more of what you know?

_____

_____

_____

_____

What kinds of struggles or fights are you facing right now in your walk with God? Are you staying pure in the midst of the struggle, keeping a clean conscience? Or is the fight causing you to compromise or surrender something you shouldn't?

_____

_____

_____

_____

Are your life and ministry balanced, or would you say they're teetering toward an extreme? What can you do to begin restoring balance?

_____

_____

_____

_____

Chapter 2: A Ministry Must Emphasize Prayer

Two key phrases about prayer emerge from chapter 2: "First of all" (v. 1) and "in every place . . . pray" (v. 8). When a ministry grows and becomes influential, we're tempted to rely on human ingenuity. We seek out brilliant minds, smart strategists, and experienced pros instead of praying.

Prayer needs to be a priority in any ministry, for what is a ministry without God's invited involvement?

◆

Is your life characterized by a constant dependence on the Lord through prayer? Or are you trying to do it all yourself?

_____

_____

_____

How about your church? Is it a praying body? Do the leaders beseech God regularly for the spiritual growth of the church, the health of our nation, and the souls of lost people? Or have human ingenuity and charisma become the fuel that drives the church?

_____

_____

_____

_____

When was the last time your church, or you personally, received a blessing that could have come no other way than from the hand of God?

Did you pray for that? Have you thanked God for providing it?

Do you see prayer as a vital link between you and God? Or has it become a rote activity, simply an obligation?

Do you invite God in on important decisions? Or is your style more "shoot from the spiritual hip"?

What do you need to do to revitalize your prayer life and reconnect with your heavenly Father? Confess a stubborn sin? Consciously develop a more grateful, praising attitude? Make prayer more spontaneous than regimented?

Chapter 3: A Ministry Must Have Qualified Leadership

The "household of God" (v. 15) is only as healthy as its leaders. That's why pastors, as well as lay leaders such as elders and deacons, must be chosen according to *scriptural* criteria, not the world's standards. Business savvy alone doesn't cut it. Slick presentation skills and charisma don't qualify a candidate for leadership.

What does? Check the home life. That's where God looks for leaders. Not the business world, but the family. Why? Because the church *is* a family. And if a man can't manage his own household, "how will he take care of the church of God?" (v. 5). We shouldn't look for perfection; even kids of the godliest leaders misbehave occasionally. The real question to ask is, "What characterizes his life?" Christian character will radiate from a candidate's relationships with family members and others.

Strong leaders make strong churches. And churches must be strong to be the pillar and support of the truth (v. 15).

◆

Are you in a position of leadership in your church? How do you measure up to the qualifications listed in 1 Timothy 3 and Titus 1? Do you see any weaknesses you need to work on?

_____

_____

_____

_____

_____

Would you be willing to commit to work on certain areas—or even resign your position—if you believed you didn't truly qualify for the position you hold?

_____

_____

_____

Who gets into leadership positions in your church? The impressive or the godly? Do spiritual qualifications supersede organizational skills? Does the selection process allow the congregation to ponder candidates and hold them to scriptural standards? Or is leadership selection simply a popularity contest?

_____

_____

_____

_____

What needs to happen in your local body to ensure the selection of godly pastors, elders, deacons, and other leaders? How can you positively contribute to that process?

_____

_____

_____

_____

Chapter 4: A Ministry Must Reflect Excellence

Jesus Christ, as the Head of the church, has included sinful humans to participate in His plan for the ages. He accomplishes His purposes by shining His strength in our weakness and displaying His triumph in the midst of our failures. But let's be careful not to use His power and mercy, or our sin, as an excuse for mediocrity. God doesn't bless laziness or halfheartedness. He is an excellent God, and our ministry should reflect His excellence.

Paul told Timothy to "take pains with these things; be absorbed in them" (v. 15), to "pay close attention" and "persevere" (v. 16). That means preachers take time to prepare excellent sermons. It means choirs strive for excellence in worship. It means we greet visitors, share our faith, support our missionaries, and teach our children with a commitment, orderliness, and passion for godliness that honors our great God.

———◆———

Are you "taking pains" with your life and ministry? If you're a Sunday school teacher, do you take time to prepare thought-provoking lessons? Or are you content to throw something together on the way to church? However you serve in the body, do you do it with a passion for excellence?

_____

_____

_____

_____

How about your own spiritual development? Have you applied yourself to that with the same vision and discipline as you do your job and your leisure activities?

_____

_____

_____

Are your public and private actions in harmony with one another? Are you a model worth following?

_____

_____

_____

_____

Often, the reason for a slippage in excellence is excessive busyness. If we try to do too much, we can end up doing everything poorly. Do you need to lop some activities off your schedule and get back to excelling in the basics?

_____

_____

_____

_____

Chapter 5: A Ministry Must Meet Needs

Chapter 5 revolves around compassion toward people—older men, younger men, older women, younger women, widows, and elders. An excellent ministry meets the needs of all kinds of people.

That means spiritual needs, such as respect, encouragement, comfort, guidance, confrontation, and dealing with sin. It also means physical needs, such as caring for the needy and paying pastoral staff. Not that ministry should be man-centered; it's God-centered. But as a church draws closer to God, it becomes aware of the deepest needs of people and the infinite resources God provides to meet them (compare 1 John 3:17–18).

◆

What need is your particular ministry meeting? The need for others to learn the Word? The need for the lost to hear the gospel? The need for the hungry to eat or the homeless to sleep? The need for others in the body to experience comfort and encouragement? The need for the church to handle its finances with integrity? Write down the need or needs God is meeting through your gifts and interests.

_____

_____

_____

_____

Does your church demonstrate compassion? Do people of all ages feel important? Are complaints heard and handled? Does your church reflect a healthy balance of helping people and magnifying God? What, if anything, would you like to see change?

_____

_____

_____

_____

Chapter 6: A Ministry Must Maintain Purity

Anyone who hasn't lived in a cave in recent years has seen enough to know that ministry can be faked; it can be done in the flesh.

But an excellent ministry, one that honors God, will exude purity; it will throb with integrity and honesty in both doctrine and personal life. Those who handle the church's funds will be accountable to others. The pastor won't be a hypocrite, preaching one way and living another. The Word will not be compromised or diluted in the name of relevance. And in the interest of maintaining a pure church, sin will be dealt with lovingly and firmly.

◆

What steps are you taking to maintain purity in your life and ministry? Are you a one-man or one-woman show, or have you surrounded yourself with others who keep you accountable?

_____

_____

_____

What about your church? Is there a dichotomy in lifestyles between Sunday and the rest of the week? Is the theology biblical? To whom are the leaders accountable? Are all the church's dealings aboveboard? Is the Word esteemed? Is Christ lifted up? What improvements can be made?

_____

_____

_____

_____

Let's Tie It All Together

As we wrap up this study of 1 Timothy, here are three final thoughts to help you keep your ministry on course.

Look up: A ministry that squares with Scripture requires consistent scriptural input. An excellent ministry feeds itself on God and His Word, maintaining pure doctrine and demonstrating complete dependence on Him. If we aren't spending time with God and His Word firsthand, we risk letting someone besides God plan our agenda.

Look within: A ministry that remains on target requires strong, internal integrity. Hand in hand with integrity is a commitment to quality—in thinking, teaching, decision making, and living for Christ. An excellent ministry requires character of its leaders and displays a commitment to godliness.

Look around: A ministry that earns the respect of others requires great personal attention. It's not enough just to teach the truth; we need to care for people. An excellent ministry lives out its theology by caring for the members of God's family.

Remember, if you're a Christian, you're a minister. Whether you're a pastor who declares the Word from the pulpit; a teenager who holds infants in the nursery; or a quiet deacon who stays behind on Sunday to clean the sanctuary: You have a ministry. God reached down to us in His grace, not just so we could be saved, but so we could be servants. Servants in our Master's household, the church.

One day our Master will return to gather His household. May He find us diligent with His affairs. After all, how can we offer less than an excellent ministry to such an excellent Savior? Serve well, fellow Christian. Serve well.

BOOKS FOR PROBING FURTHER

The letter of 1 Timothy is a banquet table of truth, adorned with good, solid food for the church of Jesus Christ. But in case you're still hungry, you might want to stock up on some of the following staples.

Character in Leadership

Getz, Gene A. *The Measure of a Man*. Ventura, Calif.: Regal Books, 1995.

Hughes, R. Kent. *Disciplines of a Godly Man*. Wheaton, Ill.: Good News Publishers, Crossway Books, 1991.

Peterson, Eugene H. *The Contemplative Pastor: Returning to the Art of Spiritual Direction*. Grand Rapids, Mich.: William B. Eerdmans Publishing Co., 1989.

————. *Working the Angles: The Shape of Pastoral Integrity*. Grand Rapids, Mich.: William B. Eerdmans Publishing Co., 1987.

The Church

Getz, Gene A. *Sharpening the Focus of the Church*. Rev. ed. Wheaton, Ill.: Scripture Press Publications, Victor Books, 1984.

Swindoll, Charles R. *The Bride: Renewing Our Passion for the Church*. Grand Rapids, Mich.: Zondervan Publishing House, 1994. Formerly titled *Rise and Shine*.

White, John, and Ken Blue. *Church Discipline That Heals*. Downers Grove, Ill.: InterVarsity Press, 1985. Formerly titled *Healing the Wounded*.

Doctrine and Theology

Boice, James Montgomery. *Foundations of the Christian Faith*. Revised in one volume. Downers Grove, Ill.: InterVarsity Press, 1986.

Erickson, Millard J. *Christian Theology*. Grand Rapids, Mich.: Baker Book House, 1985.

————. *Introducing Christian Doctrine*. Grand Rapids, Mich.: Baker Book House, 1992.

Martin, Walter. *The Kingdom of the Cults*. Rev. ed. Minneapolis, Minn.: Bethany House Publishers, 1985.

Ryrie, Charles C. *Basic Theology*. Wheaton, Ill.: Scripture Press Publications, Victor Books, 1986.

Sproul, R. C. *Essential Truths of the Christian Faith*. Wheaton, Ill.: Tyndale House Publishers, 1992.

Exposition of 1 Timothy

Barclay, William. *The Letters to Timothy, Titus, and Philemon*. Rev. ed. The Daily Study Bible series. Philadelphia, Pa.: Westminster Press, 1975.

Guthrie, Donald. *The Pastoral Epistles: An Introduction and Commentary*. 2d ed. Grand Rapids, Mich.: William B. Eerdmans Publishing Co., 1990.

Hendriksen, William. *Thessalonians, Timothy and Titus*. New Testament Commentary series. Grand Rapids, Mich.: Baker Book House, 1979.

Litfin, A. Duane. "1 Timothy." *The Bible Knowledge Commentary*. New Testament edition. Ed. John F. Walvoord and Roy B. Zuck. Wheaton, Ill.: Scripture Press Publications, Victor Books, 1983.

Pollock, John. *The Apostle: A Life of Paul*. Wheaton, Ill.: Scripture Press Publications, Victor Books, 1972.

Towner, Philip H. *1–2 Timothy and Titus*. The IVP New Testament Commentary Series. Downers Grove, Ill.: InterVarsity Press, 1994.

The Gospel

Stott, John R. W. *The Cross of Christ*. Downers Grove, Ill.: InterVarsity Press, 1986.

Materialism

Getz, Gene A. *Real Prosperity*. Chicago, Ill.: Moody Press, 1990.

Prayer

Getz, Gene A. *Praying for One Another*. Wheaton, Ill.: Scripture Press Publications, Victor Books, 1982.

Wiersbe, Warren W., comp. *Classic Sermons on Prayer*. Grand Rapids, Mich.: Kregel Publications, 1987.

Women and the Church

Mickelsen, Alvera, ed. *Women, Authority and the Bible*. Downers Grove, Ill.: InterVarsity Press, 1986.

Piper, John, and Wayne Grudem, eds. *Recovering Biblical Manhood and Womanhood: A Response to Evangelical Feminism*. Wheaton, Ill.: Good News Publishers, Crossway Books, 1991.

Some of these books may be out of print and available only through a library. For those currently available, please contact your local Christian bookstore. Books by Charles R. Swindoll may be obtained through Insight for Living. IFL also offers some books by other authors—please note the ordering information that follows and contact the office that serves you.

ORDERING INFORMATION

EXCELLENCE IN MINISTRY
Cassette Tapes and Study Guide

This Bible study guide was designed to be used independently or in conjunction with the broadcast of Chuck Swindoll's taped messages which are listed below. If you would like to order cassette tapes or further copies of this study guide, please see the information given below and the order forms provided at the end of this guide.

		U.S.	Canada
EMN	Study guide	$ 4.95 ea.	$ 6.50 ea.
EMNCS	Cassette series, includes all individual tapes, album cover, and one complimentary study guide	65.50	76.00
EMN 1–10	Individual cassettes, includes messages A and B	6.00 ea.	7.48 ea.

The prices are subject to change without notice.

EMN 1-A: *The Church as God Planned It*—A Survey of 1 Timothy
   B: *What's a Pastor to Do?*—1 Timothy 1:1–11, 18–20

EMN 2-A: *Undeserved Mercy for an Unbelieving Rabbi*— 1 Timothy 1:12–17
   B: *What's First in a Meaningful Ministry?*— 1 Timothy 2:1–4, 8

EMN 3-A: *God's Desire, Man's Debt, Christ's Payment*— 1 Timothy 2:3–7
   B: *What about Women in the Church?*—1 Timothy 2:9–15

EMN 4-A: *Checklist for Choosing Church Leaders*— 1 Timothy 3:1–7
   B: *Another Look at the Checklist*—1 Timothy 3:1–7

EMN 5-A: *The Dignity of Servanthood*—1 Timothy 3:8–13
   B: *A Hope, a House, a Hymn*—1 Timothy 3:14–16

EMN 6-A: *Ministering Amidst the Crazies*—1 Timothy 4:1–6
   B: *The Dos and Don'ts of Ministry*—1 Timothy 4:6–16

EMN 7-A: *Respecting and Rebuking the Saints*—
1 Timothy 5:1–3, 17–20
B: *What about Widows?*—1 Timothy 5:3–16

EMN 8-A: *A Prescription for Pastoral Health*—1 Timothy 5:21–25
B: *Responding Correctly to Authority*—1 Timothy 6:1–6

EMN 9-A: *Contentment . . . and How to Miss It*—
1 Timothy 6:6–10, 17–19
B: *Clear Commandments of Godliness*—1 Timothy 6:11–16

EMN 10-A: *A Treasure Worth Guarding*—1 Timothy 6:20–21
B: *Let's Evaluate Your Ministry*—A Review of 1 Timothy

How to Order by Phone or FAX

(Credit card orders only)

United States: 1-800-772-8888 from 6:00 A.M. to 4:30 P.M., Pacific time, Monday through Friday
FAX (714) 575-5496 anytime, day or night

Canada: 1-800-663-7639, Vancouver residents call (604) 532-7172 from 8:00 A.M. to 4:30 P.M., Pacific time, Monday through Friday
FAX (604) 532-7173 anytime, day or night

Australia and the South Pacific: (03) 9-872-4606 or FAX (03) 9-874-8890 from 8:00 A.M. to 5:00 P.M., Monday through Friday

---

Other International Locations: call the Ordering Services Department in the United States at (714) 575-5000 during the hours listed above.

How to Order by Mail

United States
- Mail to: Processing Services Department
  Insight for Living
  Post Office Box 69000
  Anaheim, CA 92817-0900
- Sales tax: California residents add 7.25%.
- Shipping and handling charges must be added to each order. See chart on order form for amount.
- Payment: personal checks, money orders, credit cards (Visa, Master-Card, Discover Card, and American Express). No invoices or COD orders available.
- $10 fee for *any* returned check.

Canada
- Mail to: Insight for Living Ministries
  Post Office Box 2510
  Vancouver, BC V6B 3W7
- Sales tax: please add 7% GST. British Columbia residents also add 7% sales tax (on tapes or cassette series).
- Shipping and handling charges must be added to each order. See chart on order form for amount.
- Payment: personal cheques, money orders, credit cards (Visa, MasterCard). No invoices or COD orders available.
- Delivery: approximately four weeks.

Australia and the South Pacific
- Mail to: Insight for Living, Inc.
  GPO Box 2823 EE
  Melbourne, Victoria 3001, Australia
- Shipping: add 25% to the total order.
- Delivery: approximately four to six weeks.
- Payment: personal checks payable in Australian funds, international money orders, or credit cards (Visa, MasterCard, and BankCard).

Other International Locations
- Mail to: Processing Services Department
  Insight for Living
  Post Office Box 69000
  Anaheim, CA 92817-0900
- Shipping and delivery time: please see chart that follows.
- Payment: personal checks payable in U.S. funds, international money orders, or credit cards (Visa, MasterCard, and American Express).

Type of Shipping	Postage Cost	Delivery
Surface	10% of total order*	6 to 10 weeks
Airmail	25% of total order*	under 6 weeks

*Use U.S. price as a base.

Our Guarantee

Your complete satisfaction is our top priority here at Insight for Living. If you're not completely satisfied with anything you order, please return it for full credit, a refund, or a replacement, as *you* prefer.

Insight for Living Catalog

The Insight for Living catalog features study guides, tapes, and books by a variety of Christian authors. To obtain a free copy, call us at the numbers listed above.

Order Form
United States, Australia, and Other International Locations
(Canadian residents please use order form on reverse side.)

EMNCS represents the entire *Excellence in Ministry* series in a special album cover, while EMN 1–10 are the individual tapes included in the series. EMN represents this study guide, should you desire to order additional copies.

EMN	Study guide	$ 4.95 ea.
EMNCS	Cassette series, includes all individual tapes, album cover, and one complimentary study guide	65.50
EMN 1–10	Individual cassettes, includes messages A and B	6.00 ea.

Product Code	Product Description	Quantity	Unit Price	Total
			$	$

Amount of Order	First Class	UPS		
			Order Total	
$ 7.50 and under	1.00	4.00	**UPS ❏ First Class ❏** *Shipping and handling must be added. See chart for charges.*	
$ 7.51 to 12.50	1.50	4.25	**Subtotal**	
$12.51 to 25.00	3.50	4.50	**California Residents—Sales Tax** Add 7.25% of subtotal.	
$25.01 to 35.00	4.50	4.75	**Non-United States Residents** *Australia add 25%. All other locations: U.S. price plus 10% surface postage or 25% airmail.*	
$35.01 to 60.00	5.50	5.25		
$60.00 and over	6.50	5.75		
			Gift to Insight for Living *Tax-deductible in the United States.*	

Fed Ex and Fourth Class are also available. Please call for details.

If you are placing an order after January 1, 1997, please call for current prices.

Total Amount Due *Please do not send cash.*	$

Prices are subject to change without notice.

Payment by: ❏ Check or money order payable to Insight for Living   ❏ Credit card

(Circle one):   Visa   MasterCard   Discover Card   American Express   BankCard
(In Australia)

Number _____

Expiration Date _____   Signature _____

We cannot process your credit card purchase without your signature.

Name _____

Address _____

City _____   State _____

Zip Code _____   Country _____

Telephone (____) _____   Radio Station ____ ____ ____ ____

If questions arise concerning your order, we may need to contact you.

Mail this order form to the Processing Services Department at one of these addresses:

Insight for Living
Post Office Box 69000, Anaheim, CA 92817-0900

Insight for Living, Inc.
GPO Box 2823 EE, Melbourne, VIC 3001, Australia

Order Form
Canadian Residents
(Residents of the United States, Australia, and other international locations,
please use order form on reverse side.)

EMNCS represents the entire *Excellence in Ministry* series in a special album cover, while
EMN 1–10 are the individual tapes included in the series. EMN represents this study guide,
should you desire to order additional copies.

EMN	Study guide	$ 6.50 ea.
EMNCS	Cassette series,	76.00
	includes all individual tapes, album cover,	
	and one complimentary study guide	
EMN 1–10	Individual cassettes,	7.48 ea.
	includes messages A and B	

Product Code	Product Description	Quantity	Unit Price	Total
			$	$

Amount of Order	Canada Post
Orders to $10.00	2.00
$10.01 to 30.00	3.50
$30.01 to 50.00	5.00
$50.01 to 99.99	7.00
$100 and over	Free

Subtotal	
Add 7% GST	
British Columbia Residents *Add 7% sales tax on individual tapes or cassette series.*	
Shipping *Shipping and handling must be added. See chart for charges.*	
Gift to Insight for Living Ministries *Tax-deductible in Canada.*	
Total Amount Due *Please do not send cash.*	$

Loomis is also available. Please
call for details.

*If you are placing an order after January 1,
1997, please call for current prices.*

Prices are subject to change without notice.

Payment by: ❏ Cheque or money order payable to Insight for Living Ministries
❏ Credit card

(Circle one): Visa   MasterCard   Number _____

Expiration Date _____   Signature _____
We cannot process your credit card purchase without your signature.

Name _____

Address _____

City _____   Province _____

Postal Code _____   Country _____

Telephone (____) _____   Radio Station ____ ____ ____ ____
If questions arise concerning your order, we may need to contact you.

Mail this order form to the Processing Services Department at the following address:

Insight for Living Ministries
Post Office Box 2510
Vancouver, BC, Canada V6B 3W7